To &

Jul

V

You Should Have Been Here Yesterday

By the same author

The *Sunday Express* Book
of European Holidays

LEWIS DE FRIES

You Should Have Been Here Yesterday

Robin Clark Ltd
London

First published by Robin Clark Ltd 1985
A member of the Namara Group
27/29 Goodge Street, London W1P 1FD

British Library Cataloguing in Publication Data

De Fries, Lewis
   You should have been here yesterday.
   1. Voyages and travels—1951–
   I. Title
   910.4   G465

   ISBN 0-86072-084-5

Typeset by MC Typeset, Chatham, Kent
Printed and bound in Great Britain
by Mackays of Chatham Ltd, Kent

For Jennifer

CONTENTS

FOREWORD

From the moment some idiot up front put a big inflated beachball in the overhead rack I knew exactly what would happen, even to the extent of my own involvement with the wretched thing . . . all that was needed was for the plane to give one lurch.

I found myself staring at that ball, mesmerized. But I wasn't permitted to stare for long. There was what you might call a mild diversion. Though perhaps 'mild' is not quite the word to use.

Most of my fellow-passengers – nearly all British – had been diverting themselves long before they boarded that Iberia flight from Las Palmas to Malaga, the first leg of their journey home after a Canary Islands holiday. The day had been hot, Spanish plonk was cheap, and what better way to drown sorrows at the thought of starting work next Monday . . .

Drink takes people two ways: the jolly way or the other. I was in a plane with a lot of types for whom drinking took the other course. And even those in whom it had induced some semblance of joviality at the onset of the flight soon decided – with the aid of some topping-up provided by the overworked cabin crew – to join the aggressive majority.

So when the large German lady sitting next to me turned to protest in guttural tones at a lout behind her who was expressing disgruntlement with his lot by thumping and kicking the back of her seat, the atmosphere became sour, not to say menacing.

'Drop dead, you Kraut bitch.' 'Go home, Gretel.' (Surely she was trying to do just that.)

Yobboes sitting in front turned to add to the chorus, now swelling from all directions. The victim rose in Wagnerian majesty, bellowing: 'Dis ist disgraceful!' Where, oh where were all those huge, lumbering fellow-countrymen of hers who had grabbed every available seat seconds before I reached them, whenever hunger had driven me into a restaurant at Las Palmas? Left behind on the ground, they were. The Teutonic lady was alone and defenceless among the victors of the Second World War, 30,000 feet above the Atlantic.

I would love to tell you how I leapt to her defence with old-world gallantry. But I'm not writing fiction: in real life you don't take on a planeload of unpleasant drunks. Besides, I reasoned with my conscience, amid yells of 'Bloody Germans' and 'Vait until I report dis to der Iberia', she wasn't doing too badly. I merely pressed the button for the stewardess, gritted my teeth and forced myself to stare at that damned beachball.

The stewardess came cautiously down the aisle, dark eyes wide and apprehensive. '*Señor?*' I saw her lips frame the word in the uproar. I beckoned her to lean close, put my mouth to her ear and hissed: 'Either get this lady another seat or change mine.'

'*Madre de Dios!*' she exclaimed unhelpfully. (The Spanish rise to all situations; no wonder the Armada failed.) 'Dis-a-plane is-a-full up.'

She looked desperately in all directions, as if she could conjure up an empty seat from somewhere. At that very moment, the plane lurched. And the big beachball, dislodged, sailed through the air, hit the floor, bounced, and in a sudden silence was followed by every eye as it careered down the aisle.

Of course I knew where it would stop; I had known it from the very beginning. Right at my feet. For a long moment every eye was fixed on the ball or the stewardess. Then the Spanish girl swallowed hard, turned to me and asked politely: 'Is this ball-a-yours, *señor?*'

Another roar went up, but this time it was a roar of laughter. 'Do us a favour, love,' someone shouted. 'Does 'e look the sort that carries a bloody ball abaht?'

'Yes,' I joined in, forgetting that the last thing I wanted was to be in the limelight. 'Do I look like that?' The stewardess stared at me, at my portable typewriter, at my briefcase. I wasn't exactly dressed for Threadneedle Street, but neither did I have on the regulation returning-from-a-Canary-Islands-holiday gaudy teeshirt, cotton trousers and sandals. And if I did possess a floppy sombrero, I must surely have locked it out of sight in my luggage . . .

'Er–no, *señor,*' she admitted finally. 'It's mine, Carmen,' chortled the intellectual giant who owned it, looming over her.

Somehow the tension had been defused. The Wagnerian lady, still muttering balefully, was permitted to sit unkicked for the rest of the way to Malaga, the hubbub died and there was only one snarl of, 'What sort of bloody foreign muck is this?' when lunch was served.

Nothing in fact to distract the thought now filling my mind for the first time about why I was so obviously not a returning holidaymaker. After all, if anyone on that plane should be the absolute personification of a tourist, it was I. Here I was, a professional tourist, dammit. No one had greater right – yes, I put it as strongly as that – a greater right to a sombrero, teeshirt and the rest. For what was my newspaper paying my fare to the Canaries and back – the full fare, I might say; none of these package prices including hotel, transfers and what have you – if not to report on my blissful experiences in a far-flung bit of Spain and advise others how to have an equally carefree time?

How can you tell readers about a holiday if you go lumbered with a briefcase and a typewriter? It's almost as if you are *working.* But that of course is the paradox in being a travel writer. You *are* working. Contrary to the belief of the people who read you – and even of your colleagues in other branches of journalism – the life of a travel writer can hardly be described as one long holiday.

So, as I joined the exodus from that plane at Malaga, I had somehow reconciled myself to the whole affair. To do my job properly I had to act as a tourist, think as a tourist, mingle as unostentatiously as possible with tourists. But I had always to remember that I was at the same time there on duty – and if my attendant typewriter and briefcase did not remind me of the fact, my own experience as a journalist, to say nothing of the

11

demands of my editor, would clinch matters. (I'd love to see Sir John Junor's face if I put the cost of a sombrero on my expenses.)

It's a very serious methodical business, giving advice on holidays arising from your own experiences of them. It is also very difficult explaining just what is involved personally – and I'm always astonished and flattered by the many letters people write asking about myself and my way of life. You are not necessarily moulded in your character by the job you do and other people's professions are nearly always a mystery, I suppose. You might say that to do a job like mine thoroughly and still remember it is a job I should virtually clock in for a set number of days – enjoy myself or bust.

I can only reply to that: of course I derive a lot of pleasure from my work without conscious effort or I would not still be writing about holidays after more than twenty years. But it is still hard work, and my chief relaxation has to be in my own holiday time when I make certain I do not travel at all.

What more natural? They tell me comedians are very serious chaps in their off-stage moments, while undertakers are said to be the life and soul of every jolly gathering they attend between funerals. And I hate talking shop when I'm not working: people who try to show me their colour slides taken in Majorca are positively frozen out . . . Try talking about your aches and pains to a doctor at a party.

Fortunately, I live in a lovely part of southern England, where I take my own holidays at just that time of year when everyone is rushing away on the sort of vacations I advise in my working life. It is then that I'm selfish and human enough to think smugly that there's no understanding people who want to get away from it all. But then I suppose that if I had made my home in the middle of a big city I would feel the same urge. And then it would indeed be bliss to lie in the sun or stroll to an interesting restaurant without the nagging thought that I was there to write about it.

Sometimes I think my office colleagues understand the situation less than my readers. 'How come you're not burnt black by the sun?' they demand. And nothing irritates them more when I return from my summer break and boast I've stocked the freezer with a bumper crop of wild blackberries picked yards from my front door while they are full of grievances about rain spoiling their stay in the Med.

Which brings me to the title of this book and my reason for writing it. 'You should have been here yesterday.' How often I've heard this from tourist officials when I arrive in the middle of a downpour. 'Yesterday – ah, yesterday. The weather was – fantastico! Today is freak. You have brought with you the lousy weather from England.'

I shiver, look grimly through the rain at a landscape so vividly green that the effect can be achieved only by frequent torrents and tell them: 'The weather was gorgeous at Heathrow. Not a cloud in the sky.'

'Never,' they say. 'In London it is always foggy or raining. But yesterday here – perfection! Tomorrow again it will be beautiful.' It amazes me how people in the tourist business believe their own propaganda.

And the aim of this book? To tell you some of my experiences that don't reach the travel page. Perhaps because I don't have room for them; perhaps, too, because what happens to someone like myself who travels alone and has specialized aims and requirements is not necessarily typical of what might befall the average tourist. (And the day I forget that I'm writing for Mr and Mrs Smith I might just as well change my profession.)

But principally because the purpose of travel writing is basically serious and informative and this book is merely to entertain: a professional traveller's light-hearted view of the tourist world.

I've never belonged to the school of what I would call poker-faced travel writing as practised by the heavier counterparts of the *Sunday Express*, with their hint that of course you have travelled the world and speak umpteen languages or you wouldn't be buying the paper anyway. Or written with the assurance that you are one with the writer when he starts a languid piece with: 'When I was last in Kuala Lumpur . . .'

Nor, thank heaven, have I had the luxury of so much space that my *Sunday Express* page is a guidebook in miniature: 'Turn left into the Grand Place and there's the statue of that great old

Archbishop Wittgenstein who died full of honours in 1187.' The bookshops are crammed with heavy tomes packed with that sort of stuff.

Perhaps, though, I'm being unfair to myself. This book does set out to be a sort of guide, based on my personal experiences, to prepare you for situations that can arise at any time you leave these shores.

How, for example, to know what to do when offered a hedgehog as a bribe on the fringes of the Sahara. The correct procedure when dealing with a professional Arab assassin who phones you at midnight when you are alone in a Moroccan hotel. How to react when you find yourself the cause of a near riot on a Norwegian mountain peak. The proper behaviour when your hostess at a posh San Francisco restaurant collapses drunkenly face down in her dish of roast duck – and stays there. How to persuade the Spanish Post Office that Leatherhead actually exists. The perfect way to make a clumsy ass of yourself at a ritual Japanese tea ceremony. What happens when you lose your spectacles in Peking, when a turkey attacks you in the middle of the Sea of Galilee. And when a package of volcanic ash, sent to you by a grateful Italian island for an article you have written, leaks on top of the bowler hat of a gentleman all unknowingly reading *The Times* on a train about to stop at Surbiton.

You cannot escape the fact that sooner or later in your travels you will meet situations like these. I guarantee that this is the first book ever printed which tells you how to deal with them.

For if you can't you might as well tear up your passport and follow King George V's footsteps to Bognor this summer. See you there . . .

You Should Have Been Here Yesterday

1

STERN AND WILD
Scotland

In my pre-Fleet Street days working as a Surrey bi-weekly's only Jewish reporter, I was intrigued to find myself regarded as an ethnic oddity and apparently the nearest thing to a Roman Catholic in the office. Automatically I was given all assignments with a Catholic connection, including the highly responsible, rewarding task of standing on church steps – usually in torrential rain – and taking the names of mourners pouring out from funeral services. As the vast majority muttered their names to me over their shoulders in heavy Irish accents and were swallowed up in the throng before I could ask them to repeat themselves, I invariably had the wrong spelling – with the result that on publication day they would phone to complain and the editor would sigh and frown at me and plainly wonder why the Vatican had not supplied him with someone more reliable.

I was even despatched early one morning to the first ever nuns' initiation ceremony to be held in public at the local convent, to sit there hour by hour with incense shaken over me while the bishop snipped a symbolic lock from the head of each gowned young novice kneeling before him. Whether the editor's nerve broke when my story appeared in proof form and he appealed to the convent for verification of my facts, or whether the Mother Superior had decided on her own initiative that the press representative was plainly out of his depth and censorship was required, I shall never know. But I was summoned to the editor's office to stand respectfully beside the

17

result of my efforts while the Mother Superior and her acolytes, habits rustling, bent over the proofs and murmured in soft, depracatory tones: 'No, Oi don't tink that's quoite right. What the bishop meant t'was this . . . '

Things were very different in sophisticated Fleet Street, however, Admittedly I was still regarded as an ethnic oddball, but my religious horizons were broadened to embrace all Christianity. I was now, it seemed, the nearest thing to a Christian in sight.

Though there was perhaps the faintest twinkle in the eye of my first London features editor on the day he told me: 'Do us a six-parter, old man, interviewing well-known people on "Why I believe in Jesus".'

After that, there seemed nothing in the way of my attaining the heights of religious reporting. I was sent to interview the Archbishop of Canterbury himself. It was, admittedly, to ask the daftest question I've ever had to put in my professional career: 'If life is discovered on other planets, what would be the attitude of the Church of England?'

Lord Fisher rose to the occasion magnificently. After the merest twitch of his lips, he intoned: 'My dear young man. So long as that life is more than just seaweed, of course we should evangelize.' My piece made the leader page of the *Daily Express* and the powers that be were full of praise.

So, as the time approached for me to change from a mixture of general features and travel pieces to full-time travel journalism, I was not surprised to be told to do a colour piece on the tiny Scottish island of Iona, a rugged spot off the shores of Mull, a holy isle and a pilgrimage centre throughout centuries of Christendom. From Iona, I learnt as I did my pre-trip homework, St Columba's disciples sallied forth to win the hearts of the mainland heathen. Plainly I was the man for the job.

It was going to be a big production. They even sent a photographer with me. He was known as Jock, but he was about as Scottish as I was. He was also an anti-smoking fanatic and he had the upper hand because it was his own minute Beetle car that was decreed to take us northwards. We got on reasonably well, but the journey was cramped, interminable and for me particularly nerve-racking – for in times of stress and, even more, of downright boredom, my pipe is indispensable.

At each halt I would puff away frantically – which is no way to enjoy good tobacco – while he regarded the smoke-clouds with distaste. The further north we went the more our mood darkened. There was the food for one thing: it grew progressively worse. For me it reached its nadir in one dour establishment where the meal was so appalling that I felt compelled to tell the manager so.

He looked outraged, rushed away and returned with a yellowing press cutting in a fly-blown frame. It eulogized the restaurant and the byline was that of a plainly disinterested, unprejudiced party: Hector Mac-someone-or-other.

'Do you know who this man is?' he demanded.

'A Scot?' asked Jock innocently.

'No less a person,' the manager grated on, 'than the travel editor of the Scottish *Sunday Express*. It just shows that experts – real experts – know good food when they eat it.'

Now readers often ask me whether I preserve my anonymity in restaurants I write about as, I am told, do the inspectors representing the more scrupulous good-food guides. Or whether I reveal I'm a journalist and risk out-of-the-ordinary treatment.

My reply is that to admit I'm writing for a newspaper would be the height of irresponsibility. I could never be sure that what they were giving me was not something special to impress me and that this would be denied to any reader who followed up my advice and chose the same restaurant.

But in this particular instance there was no longer any point in concealment; in fact it was my duty to tell the restaurant manager that he could not possibly still any criticism he might receive by using my own newspaper's ancient account of his splendid cuisine.

'Whoever this Hector Mac-someone is,' I told him, 'he wrote it all a long time ago, certainly not during my years on the paper. This story does not represent the current opinion of Express Newspapers, so kindly don't conceal the faults of your place behind it.'

Feeling triumphant and self-righteous, we paid our bill and, leaving the manager speechless, marched out to our tiny car. But our satisfaction at the impact we had caused all too soon evaporated. For it wasn't only poor food which dogged our progress north to the holy isle of Iona; it was also the worsening weather.

We must have been mad, I told Jock, not to kick like hell at the idea of going to Scotland so early in the year. True, down south there had been a hint of spring in the air, even though Easter hadn't arrived. But north of the border winter was still raging – it rained with a savage intensity, the wind blew the little car all over the road and I shuddered to think of the sea crossing ahead.

We left Jock's car at Oban, had a wretched passage to Mull, where a bus which had known better days – Flanders, 1914? – rattled us across the island to the far shore. There a cosy open launch waited to throw us from one wave-top to another with occasional slides down the troughs between, on the last leg of our journey to St Columba's sacred island.

With typical Sassenach arrogance – not my description but that of our welcoming hostess in this fount of Christianity – we had not booked hotel rooms. Our Scottish mentors back in Fleet Street had said there was no point because no one went to Iona so early in the year. And our first sight of the place under a black sky and being pounded in a gale presented us with a scene and an atmosphere which only hair-shirted masochists could possibly have enjoyed.

All we wanted now was a drink, a hot bath, a good dinner and a comfortable bed. But what no one had allowed for was – a Highland wedding. This welcome news was given to us with a good deal of relish by the owner of the one hotel actually open; every room was taken. She herself represented the second nasty surprise we had suffered when we set foot on Iona soil. She was elderly, bedraggled – and very drunk indeed. Standing there, each in our little pools of rain and seawater dripping on to the threadbare foyer carpet, Jock and I looked at her aghast.

It wasn't so much her appearance and condition that knocked us back – not we hardy types who know pre-Xmas Fleet Street – but her positively demoniacal joy in telling us: 'Serve ye right

20

for not booking. There's just the floor to sleep on when everyone's gone to their beds. If ye don't like it there's always the beach.'

Now there are colleagues I've told about our Iona adventure who have replied loftily that they would never have accepted such a state of affairs – particularly when the old hag threatened to charge us the normal room rate for a night on the lounge floor. Not them – they would have marched out into the night and gone from cottage to cottage until some kind Christian soul relented and provided a bed.

I'd have liked to see them try. Nothing would have induced Jock and me, soaked and tired as we were, to plunge back into the hell outside on the slender chance that if we hadn't broken our ankles on the rough path or fallen over a cliff in the stygian blackness, we would eventually have found bed and board somewhere.

'We'll take the floor,' I said resignedly.

'Then ye'll have to make yourselves useful,' said this member of the cast of *Macbeth*. She thrust an axe at an open-mouthed Jock and ordered: 'Ye can chop some wood for the kitchen fire.' And turning to me she rapped: 'And ye'll put mah stockings on for me; I've a hell of a sore heid and canna bend doon.'

For one wild moment – and I know the thought occurred to Jock too – I was tempted to tell her to go to hell and take my chances outside. But a particularly savage blast of wind struck the old building at that instant and I caved in. Jock, shaking his head in dazed fashion, was thrust out of the back door to the wood pile. And I – feeling the whole affair was some ghastly nightmare – found myself kneeling on the flagged kitchen floor while the virago thrust a not too clean foot in my face.

I made a clumsy job of it – my hands were chilled for one thing, and for another I was hardly encouraged by the storm of criticism she directed at me: 'God, man, have ye never put a woman's stockings on for her? Don't ye know that the pointed end goes on the bloody toes?'

I gritted my teeth and persisted. The thought of that beach was terrifying. But I also made up my mind that beach or no beach, the whole exercise would be abandoned if she insisted on my fastening those stockings at the top end. Thank God she didn't.

Somehow I completed the task. She stood up, swaying slightly. 'Ye've earned a scone for yer tea,' she said. She staggered across the kitchen, picked up a butter dish and promptly dropped it on the floor, shattering it. 'Deerie deerie me,' she moaned. 'Will ye just look at that? It's mah heid tha's awfu' bad.'

Once again, the prospects of a night in the open crossed my mind. If, I reasoned, she cut her stockinged feet on those fragments of pottery she'd blame me and that would be that. I bent down, started collecting the remains of the butter dish – and promptly gashed my finger. I suppressed an oath – this was, after all, a holy island. But the resident of Iona swaying before me was less particular. 'Dammit,' she screeched. 'I've never met anyone so ham-handed in all mah bloody life.'

At that moment Jock staggered in from the gale with an armful of firewood. His jaw sagged at the scene: spots of my blood on the floor, me clutching my bleeding finger amid the debris, and the old woman still swaying as though in time to the gale, telling me off.

Now she directed her drunken impatience at him. 'Put that stuff on the fire, man, don't just stand there.' Jock looked at me, shrugged and obeyed orders.

But she wasn't satisfied with the results of his efforts. 'Call that a bloody fire?' she howled. She picked up a pan of frying oil and emptied it on top of the big open range. Transfixed, Jock and I watched a sheet of flame roar up to the ceiling, adding to the black stains which must have been accumulating for decades . . .

If that hotel had been a comparatively flimsy modern building and not one apparently designed to withstand the combined hordes of Montrose and Claverhouse, not to mention Black Douglas, Rob Roy and Bonnie Prince Charlie, that would have been the end of the saga. It would have meant a night on the beach all right, but now in company with the roofless hostess and her equally deprived guests. . . a fearful prospect.

All that happened, however, was that the flames eventually

died down to be replaced by acrid smoke which sent us all reeling and coughing into the bar, now rapidly filling with kilted toughs arriving for the celebrations.

A ghastly evening followed: someone bandaged my finger and Jock and I were allowed a table corner for what Samuel Pepys would have described as a nasty dinner. We made ourselves as inconspicuous as possible while the drinking, dancing, leering, groping and yelling went on. Only after the last retching guest had staggered off to bed were we allowed to take over the lounge which looked as though a bomb had hit it.

A miserable fire was dying in the grate – and there was no sign of anything to replenish it. 'Don't ask me to go out with an axe again,' Jock said, between gritted teeth. There wasn't even a blanket to spare, it seemed. I huddled on the floor in my duffel coat, a cushion under my head. Jock stretched out on two hard chairs. The rest of the chairs in the lounge looked just as hard; I decided he was welcome to them.

I woke up shivering. Then to my joy I saw a brightness on the sea through the window. The sun was up, thank God. Jock was snoring still, the hotel was hushed. I found my chilly way to the bathroom, stripped, turned on the shower tap marked 'Hot' and was drenched in an icy deluge. I used language which would have shocked St Columba, shaved, dressed and returned to the lounge through the still sleeping hotel.

I felt like kicking the snoring Jock awake. Then a nasty thought struck me. Why had no one moved in the whole place? And why was it no lighter outside? I peered through the window and saw to my horror that the moon and not the sun was shining on the sea. The stars were out, too. I grabbed my watch from the table – and my heart sank. Twenty to three.

I'll never know how I got through the rest of that long night. There was certainly no question of being able to go back to sleep.

When the wedding guests dispersed next day, the harridan graciously allowed us bedrooms for the rest of our stay. I didn't think the beds were much more comfortable than the floor, but I felt so bruised and battered that I would probably have been restless in a bed in Holyrood House.

On the morning we finally left St Columba's island paradise

to catch the early launch to Mull I gave vent to my feelings by slamming the hotel front door behind me – a fact duly reported by the old woman to my bemused editor. ('She writes that you woke the whole place,' he told me. 'Good,' I said. 'It would almost be worth going back there just for the pleasure of slamming the door again.')

Damp, red-eyed – me brooding over the task of trying to write a piece and Jock feeling savage that the weather hadn't been conducive to taking reasonable photographs – we crossed to and over Mull in grim silence and piled into that tiny car on the Oban quayside for the journey south.

'I was trying to remember,' I said after a few miles, 'who said that the best thing about Scotland was the road to England.'

Jock grunted. 'Whoever he was, he had a point,' he muttered. Then he glared at me. 'What are you patting your pockets for? For God's sake don't say you left something behind in that hell-hole.'

'If I don't smoke,' I said weakly, 'I'll die. After that experience – '

'You're not puffing that sodding pipe in my car!'

I tried one last ploy. 'You anti-smokers are in good Scottish company,' I told him. 'James I was always ranting on about the evils of tobacco.'

But I was wasting my breath.

'Light that bloody thing – and you can walk home!'

2

LIFE WITH THE LATINS
France, Spain, Portugal and Italy

A reader once wrote asking me which country I found the most difficult to work in. The question jolted me somewhat – during the years I've come to anticipate virtually every question reaching my desk: 'Do you really go on these tours yourself?' 'Are you paid by travel agents?' 'What's your own favourite country?' 'Is Greece any good?' 'Where would you go if you were in my situation?' And so on.

But the most difficult country to work in? I had to think furiously about that. But not for long. And the answer I gave must have raised eyebrows. No – not some obscure banana republic; not a dour People's Paradise behind the Iron Curtain. Or even Darkest Africa. Although all these have given me some problems in my time.

The answer is – Spain. The spot on the globe which sees more visitors from Britain than any other, where you can't see the beaches because they are hidden under hundreds of thousands of British bottoms, where signs reading, 'Fish and Chips like Mother makes' proliferate, where runways are crammed with British charter flights for so much of the year.

I can't really explain why. Perhaps it is because the Spanish are so used to us that there is a certain could-not-care-less contempt in their familiarity; perhaps because their country sells itself so effortlessly that they have given up trying hard enough. Perhaps, too, that it is partly my own fault: I went there for the first time with non-existent Spanish expecting too much because the path was so well-trodden.

25

But the fact remains that Spain is the only country I have ever visited where, in distress at losing my luggage, I appealed to airport officials for help in tracing it, only to be met by a muttered, 'It is not-a-my-a problem, *señor*. It is-a-your-a problem.' The fact is, too, that so many Spaniards I have met in the tourist business have a grasp of English about equivalent to mine of Spanish. And that is more of a blow to someone like myself who needs facts, figures and detailed information than to a tourist whose requirements are less demanding and who in any event has more leisure to absorb the place.

I once said as much to the Spanish Tourist Office in London and, suitably moved, they promised that next time I would have the exclusive services of their best English-speaking driver-guide from Madrid. He met me at Bilbao; he was friendly, interested and anxious to please. And his English was hopeless.

'I been England, *señor*,' he said.

'Oh, where?' I asked.

'Truffle on Onions, *señor*.' (This is no exaggeration.)

'*Where?*'

'Truffle on Onions.'

I stared at him. 'A truffle,' I said slowly, 'is a vegetable dug up by pigs and regarded as a delicacy. Onions used to be sold in strings by continentals cycling around England. You can't make a decent tortilla without them. But I don't recognize Truffle on Onions as a place.'

He looked pained and astonished. 'But, *señor*,' he protested. 'Truffle on Onions – boning place of Cesspit.'

My head began to ache. 'A cesspit,' I explained patiently, 'is a tank used for sewage by people not fortunate enough to be on main drains. A boning place is, I suppose, an abattoir where they slaughter animals.'

He plainly thought I was raving mad. '*Señor* – William Cesspit.'

'Who?'

'William Cesspit, your famous poet.'

'Oh God,' I said. 'You mean Shakespeare – William Shakespeare. You don't mean boning place – you mean birthplace. And Truffle on Onions is Stratford-upon-Avon.'

26

He beamed. 'Right, *señor*. Truffle on Onions, boning place of Cesspit.'

It isn't only their awful English, either – there's the national Spanish pastime of making bureaucracy the excuse for sheer bloody-mindedness: combine the two and the result is chaos. I was once unfortunate enough (but only in this particular context) to live in a part of Surrey where the nearest large town was Leatherhead. I shall never understand why – but the word 'Leatherhead' when written on a telegram form at post offices in Latin countries like Spain, Portugal and Italy, would inevitably result in blank looks across the counter, a shrug from the clerk and a refusal to accept the message for transmission.

'Dis-a town Lee-i-cherheerda – it no exist.'

'Nonsense. Thousands of people live there as well as me.'

'I look in-a da book. Every town of Inglaterra, it 'as. No town a-lika-dis.'

'Look – you send it. British Post Office find it.' (This with raised voice, as usual when speaking pidgin English to thick natives who don't understand us.)

'Impossible, *señor* (or *senhor*, or *signore*). If it is a-not in-a da book me no send.'

Resignedly I would produce extra pesetas (or lire, or escudos). 'Ah, Lee-i-cherheerda. I find OK.'

I had actually planned to move to a more comprehensible address (Haslemere couldn't be quite so bad, I thought) when I found myself one night in Las Palmas. Too tired to take the telegram to the post office myself, I despatched a boy from the hotel. It did not cross my mind that somewhere so sophisticated, so tourist-orientated as Las Palmas could give me any trouble. But I was wrong.

I was just settling down to sleep when the phone rang. If I could only have taken a tape recording of that conversation I would have been a wow in show business.

'Dis is a-da Post Office. Dis-a town in Inglaterra. It no exist.' Here we went again.

'Look,' I said, wearily, 'it does exist. And you are going to damnwell send that telegram.'

'Impossible, *señor*. Not in-a da book.'

'I'm not going to get dressed and come round to argue with you,' I told him. 'Send the bloody thing. They'll know what to do with it in England.'

'You must-a spell dis-a word, *señor*.'

'But I have spelt it – read it for yourself.'

'You must-a spell it-a again.'

'L-E-A-T-H-E-R-H-E-A-D,' I recited.

'No, *señor*. No understand. Must spell like alphabet.'

Now what? They'd never understand it the English way: 'L for London, E for Edward, A for apple . . .' I'd have to try to do it in Spanish.

'OK,' I said. 'Here goes. L for Las Palmas.'

'L for Las Palmas, *señor*. Very good.'

I went on, with the clerk repeating every letter after me.

'E for Espagna, A for Andalusia, T for Toledo, H for . . .' I petered out. I couldn't think of a damned Spanish word beginning with H.

Knowing with a sinking heart that our 'H' sound is the Spanish 'J', but reckoning on one letter being wrong making little difference when the message reached England, I spluttered: 'Haitch, Haitch, H.'

'No understand. What is-a-dis "Haitch"?'

'Oh, for heaven's sake,' I yelled. 'You have the letter in front of you, man.'

'Calm, *señor*. Ah . . . H for Honda, *si*?'

I wasn't thinking of Japanese cars at the time. Perhaps Honda was a Spanish word I didn't know. Anyway, it sounded vaguely Spanish . . .

'H for Honda,' I said. I continued: 'E for Espagna, R for Roberto. H for Honda, whatever Honda means.'

And the voice of Spanish bureaucracy repeated after me, like a parrot: 'H for Honda – whatever Honda means.'

I reckoned it took about twenty minutes to get that blasted town name over to Las Palmas Post Office. We were stuck on the last letter, too. Nothing in Spanish beginning with D came to mind.

'No understand dis Dee Dee Dee. Calm, *senor*. A moment. . . ah, *si*, D is for Denmark, *si*?'

28

'I was trying to do it in Spanish,' I roared. 'You're on the international code. You understood me all the time, didn't you?'

'*Si, señor.*'

'Then why make me go into all this?'

'Regulations, *señor.*'

See what I mean? Needless to say, I changed my address.

Perhaps I'm being unfair to Spain – a country for which, despite all I've said, I do retain some kindly feelings – by including this next small tale in the chapter of Spanish mishaps. In all justice, I can't blame anyone but myself for what happened; but as you will see, there was some Spanish connection. In any event, take it as an example of the risks of writing for a mass-circulation market: make one slip and the consequences can be awkward, to say the least.

Back in the bad old days of the £50 travel allowance, I was hard put to find destinations where the costs involved did not exceed the limit. The most obvious example which came to mind was a ten-day cruise on a Spanish banana boat to the Canaries and back for what even in those times was a highly reasonable all-in figure of £68. If you bought this cruise, too, you barely dented your precious allowance: only £5 of the total charged was payable in pesetas. Sterling, naturally unlimited, covered the rest.

For a reason I cannot now remember, I omitted from the foot of the article the usual note for enquirers to apply to the Spanish National Tourist Office for further details. This was to prove disastrous. With no idea of what shipping company was involved – we did not name it in the piece to avoid the impression that it was a form of advertising – and bursting against the £50 allowance restraint in the first winter it was applied, thousands of people wrote and telephoned the office. In fact, my mailbag in three days totalled some 12,000 letters about this wretched banana-boat cruise.

My boss, the formidable Caledonian John Junor, was outraged at the costly effort we would have to make to observe the strict office rule that all readers' letters must be answered.

'Do you realize, Lewis,' he rasped, 'that it means 12,000 pieces of paper, 12,000 stamps, 12,000 envelopes – not to say typists' time?' I realized it all too well: I was as unpopular with my secretary over the affair as I was with the editor and the telephone switchboard operators.

I was in London for only a couple of rushed days between trips and tried in my short amount of free time to make amends. I called on the services of the typing pool, had three stencils cut, each answering one of the three main groups of readers' questions. Each stencil bore the name and address of the shipping company. But in my hurry I did not check one of them carefully enough. If I had I would have noticed that by some trick of ill luck, two digits of the company's telephone number had been placed in the wrong order.

So the letters went out and I disappeared abroad, relieved that the crisis had apparently been solved. How wrong I was! I returned eventually to find chaos raging: it transpired that 4,500 letters had been despatched bearing the number of a French-run ladies' hairdressing salon.

The recipients rang the office, furious. My secretary was on the verge of resigning, the switchboard people were after my blood – and the editor demanded to see me almost before I took off my coat.

'Lewis, what the hell do you mean by it? We've got to apologize to all these people. And that means 4,500 pieces of paper, 4,500 stamps, 4,500 envelopes . . .' How I wished I had stayed abroad.

Then Madame Fifi phoned – and I had to hold the headpiece away from my ear. Unlike all the other callers, the last thing she wanted was to take a cruise in a banana boat to the Canaries. In fact, the very last subject she wished to hear about was that cruise.

'I am obliged, *m'sieur*,' she screamed, 'to go to a public telephone box to call you as an escape from my own phone. My numbair is engaged day and night with your readers asking for a banana-boat cabin. It is quite disgusting.'

'I agree, *madame*,' I said, helplessly. 'I can only apologize – '

'Apologize? What is the use of that, *m'sieur*? The damage has been done. Heaven knows how much business has been lost by my clients being unable to book appointments. I shall consult my solicitors.'

Once again, I wished I had stayed abroad. But Madame Fifi was not finished with me. Despite my embarrassment over the whole absurd affair, I couldn't help being intrigued as, with true French business sense, she told me how she had at least tried to make best of an opportunity to be in contact with a wider section of the great British public than normally fell to her lot.

'I told them,' she rattled on, 'the truth: "This is not a banana-boat booking agency, but a hairdressing salon. Why not have your hair done instead?" '

'And what was their response to that?' I asked.

'Pouff!' The traditional Gallic expression of contempt came down the wire with explosive force. I held the phone ever further from my ear.

'They said, *m'sieur*, "We don't want our bloody hair done. We want to go on a banana boat. You know what you can do with your bloody haircuts." *Mon Dieu*, what terrible people read your newspaper, *m'sieur*. The Spanish banana people can 'ave them, so far as I'm concerned. But, *m'sieur*, do you know what made me even more mad? When I told them they had the wrong numbair, they said: "Impossible. The *Sunday Express* 'as given us this numbair . . . it must be the right one!" Tell me, are you infallible? The Pope or even Jesus Christ?'

She slammed down the phone at that point. If she had given me a chance to tell her so I would have pointed out that I was somewhat short of standards of divine infallibility. But I think she guessed that already.

'Come, *monsieur*,' said Madame La Baronne, with all the graciousness of the old French aristocracy, 'and I will conduct you to the cloakroom in person.' She put on a thick expensive-looking fur coat. 'And you will need to wrap up warm, I fear,' she added, as she picked up a torch.

I was incredulous. Surely in this great pinnacled, castellated *château* in the heart of France, where I was to dine with the descendants of the Mighty Unguillotined, the loo was not at the bottom of the garden?

31

I was even more startled when she added: 'You will never find your way back alone, so I shall wait to escort you. I really do not mind, *monsieur*. I am used to this with strangers.'

Still in disbelief, I followed her. But not outside. Instead she led me from the vast hall with its roaring log fire, up a majestic staircase, along a gallery filled with portraits of her disapproving-looking ancestors, lined with tapestries, suits of armour and battleaxes; then up another great staircase and along another seemingly endless gallery and so to a tiny door set in the circular landing of a turret, which she opened with a courtly flourish. I reckoned the journey from fireplace to lavatory door took a full five minutes. And by heavens, it was cold.

I had tried to memorize the route – there seemed something almost bizarre in the idea of a baroness in her own *château* waiting humbly on the freezing ill-lit landing outside the door while I flushed the loo and washed my hands. 'I'm sure I can get back to the hall alone, *madame*,' I ventured.

But she was adamant. 'Impossible, *monsieur*,' she said. 'People have been lost before in this house.' The remark conjured up visions of hapless guests, confused in the maze of corridors, staircases and armoured knights, wandering until dawn, while far below them in the great hall dinner grew cold and there would be talk of search parties. Perhaps those great chests lining the galleries were full of bones of wayfarers, who fell exhausted into their cavernous depths, the iron-bound lids clicking firmly shut after them and their frantic knockings unheard until doomsday . . .

I decided not to argue. Looking back on it, I don't think I could have managed that journey back to the warmth of the only fire in the mighty pile without an escort, however distinguished.

What a relief it all was – to take off my overcoat again and warm my hands by the blaze, a place being found for me amid sympathetic murmurs of fellow-guests – I could have been Amundsen returning from beating Scott to the South Pole.

There wasn't anyone there – except myself, of course – under the rank of *vicomte*. The French are such sturdy republicans and Robespierre and Co made such a thorough job of the

Revolution, that you tend to think the bluebloods were creatures of the past. But that night I found they were still thick on the ground in Mitterrand's Socialist France.

A large percentage of the Revolution's survivors had gathered in the baroness's *château* to dine in my honour. Perhaps that is making the occasion sound rather grander than it was: they were actually there on a strict matter of business. The local tourist authorities – over whom the grandees held a remarkable amount of sway – had informed them that I was touring the area to write a piece about its holiday possibilities – so they leapt at the chance to meet me.

They were there to sell their *châteaux* to the readers of the *Sunday Express* through me: the only way they could keep the great places up, they had decided, was to take a leaf from the book of their British counterparts and invite paying guests. Perhaps I could help them find the means of lighting more than one fire. (You would imagine, by the way they huddled around the baroness's flaming log pile in the hall, that hers was the only fire in the whole *département*. Perhaps it was – perhaps it was *her* night to use the bellows.)

Guiltily I wondered if I should venture to point out that even in the middle of a heatwave, I would lose readers from pneumonia if I advocated bed and breakfast in such a *château*. But I reasoned the likely reply to that would be: 'Send us guests, *monsieur*, and we will have the means to heat our castles.' As I've observed before, they are marvellously practical business types, the French.

Time for dinner and I found myself seated at the widest longest table I've ever sat at in my life. Tactfully they placed me on the side nearer the fire – the poor devils opposite must have been frozen to their chairs.

I was certain by now that there wouldn't be any liveried flunkeys in attendance. So I wasn't surprised by the sight of one aged retainer hobbling in to serve us all, and because of the number of guests around that table and the sheer awkwardness of its length and width, it took an age for her to fill our plates. I was served first, and by the time everyone was ready to start the food was cooling rapidly. To get at the solitary salt and pepper set was hard work in itself. The sender had to lean as far as

33

possible towards you, push it across the table, while you, leaning towards him with hands outstretched, could just about grasp it.

I had also given up all hope of *haute cuisine*. It was a simple meal – charcuterie, quiche, guineafowl, cheese and chocolate mousse – as would have been served to you in any of the country restaurants around. The wine, too, was nothing to get excited about; it just suited the food. All pleasant enough, but not what you would have called gracious *château*-style living.

What astonished me, though, was that with the exception of the mousse, *each course was served on the same plate*. Was it to wring my heart, I wondered. Were *Les Bailiffs* even now in the kitchen seizing the rest of the crockery? Was it a desperate race against time, this attempt to fill the echoing rooms, galleries and halls with *Sunday Express* readers, before seals were placed on the great doors and the erstwhile occupants were ejected shivering into the night, their titles their only possessions? The mind boggled.

'I will put on the light for you to find your way out of the courtyard,' the baroness said when she wished me *bon voyage*. I had visions of one tiny pinprick of light to see me on my way across the flagstones, the gravel, through the narrow archway, over the drawbridge and down the long drive to the edge of the vast park.

I turned up my headlights as soon as I started my car. But the impoverished aristocrats of Central France had one more surprise in store for me that night. The baroness pressed a switch – and that mighty façade with its buttresses, its turrets, its battlemented walls, sprang into blazing light from hundreds of bulbs. It must have cost the earth to see me off.

It is a pretty poor sort of travel article which features France and makes no mention of food – and not just because the most commonplace dishes sound marvellous in a language that appears to have been created just for them. The sheer delight of eating in France is such an integral part of a holiday there that if I did not dwell lovingly on some of the feasts I have enjoyed on the other side of the Channel I just wouldn't be doing my job

34

properly. There are readers, of course, who write scathingly that they wish I would stop drooling about French *cuisine*, that it takes away their appetite for Sunday lunch, and did I know that while travelling around France on my stomach I was ignoring the plight of starving millions? (There is of course one consolation: if there should be another Civil War in this country you'd know the sort of people who would take the Roundhead side.)

But far, far more write to say that they drool with me and what was the name of that lovely little restaurant I described in the Dordogne? In fact, I probably get more letters about eating in France than on any other single subject. And I've yet to have one telling me off for ignoring *nouvelle cuisine*.

This is, it seems, a cult with origins in the desire of a group of pricey chefs in Lyons to set themselves up, after consultations with the Japanese, as sort of stomach doctors. Eat only a quarter of your usual amount, forget 'harmful' sauces, but pay three times as much for the privilege of having guaranteed fresh products. Beautifully presented, of course, in imitation of those dainty eaters of tiny quantities (and creators of vast amounts of washing-up) from the most distant East.

Perhaps I'm old-fashioned, but without being so Philistine as to suggest that it is quantity rather than quality that counts, I've always taken the line that one should have both. You're entitled to the best, the most satisfying food you can afford to buy and it is, after all, your own stomach, your own digestion, your choice and your taste that's involved. Chefs should stick to cooking and leave medicine to another profession who wear white coats. I see no point in going to bed hungry after paying the earth for umpteen tiny courses made up of a couple of peas, a baby courgette, a transparently thin piece of duck and a child's portion of sorbet, however tastefully presented.

I've tried in vain to persuade the French tourist authorities to print a special symbol beside names of restaurants specializing in *nouvelle cuisine* so that those who actually want to eat something can go elsewhere. Each time I have been greeted with expressions of Gallic horror. Restaurants, even those passionately believing in the cult – and presumably laughing all the way to the bank as a result – would never stand for it. In any event, they say, a study of the menu in advance will show the discerning and the experienced just what sort of food is being provided.

That means, so far as I am concerned, that in this matter of choosing the right restaurant to suit yourself, you are strictly on your own. The clues alleged to be contained in the printed menus – especially in the more scanty ones provided on the outside of the restaurant rather than within – are too subtle for most of us, if they exist at all.

So let me give you a word of warning: if for some reason, as was the case with me recently, you are not sufficiently hungry to tackle what appears to be an endless fixed menu and ask instead for one dish *à la carte*, demand in the first place to know whether they are serving *nouvelle cuisine* or normal food. Otherwise you might find yourself, as I did, contemplating in rage and incredulity a child-size portion dwarfed by the immense plate on which it came, provided at a price almost equal to the entire fixed menu.

At least, when you are on your own feet, you can pick and choose where to eat. But what on earth do you do if, captive as I was once, aboard the most publicized luxury train in Europe, you take your seat in the dining-car, are told there is no alternative to the admittedly mammoth-sounding fixed menu (terrifyingly priced and an extra to the even more terrifying train fare) and having ordered it, find yourself confronted with *nouvelle cuisine* at its most scanty?

At the end of it all – 'all', did I say? – I beckoned the dignified head waiter and asked for a Mars bar.

'*Monsieur!*' He was so shocked that he could utter no other word.

'I'm still hungry,' I said.

He recovered his speech. 'But *monsieur* has had the whole menu!'

'And *monsieur* is still hungry,' I said. 'So what about a Mars?' (I'd hate to think what it would have cost, even if he could have found one in the pantry. A cup of muddy coffee cost fifteen French francs at the time and heaven only knows what it is now.)

I watched him depart on his impossible errand and had the

36

distinct impression that he would not try to find a Mars bar. In fact, I was sure I would never see him again until the train's apology for breakfast – and I didn't. But my vain gesture in taking the anti-*nouvelle cuisine* campaign deep into the enemy camp, as it were, had not gone unnoticed.

A small lady at a nearby table leaned over conspiratorially and hissed: 'I quite agree with you. I'm thinking of signing a petition against the food.'

'Draw it up and I'll sign it,' I told her. 'We should head it: "From the Hungry Ones".'

We exchanged names and her eyebrows went up. 'I always read you,' she said. 'Do you mean to say you can't do anything about it?'

'I'm a fare-paying passenger just like you,' I told her. 'All I can do is pretend that the damned train doesn't exist.'

My practice is not to write a piece if I decide that the snags, whatever they are, outweigh the advantages to a tourist. I regard that as being as good a principle as any.

But I rate food – especially in France – as so important to the success of a holiday, that even if I had no other grumbles about that much-publicized luxury train (still running and doing fabulously well, apparently) nothing would have induced me to write favourably about it. The fact that I did have a lot of other faults to find was, if you like, a sort of bonus in reverse.

I have often wondered since if a Hungry Ones petition had any success. The price of that train trip has now reached such heights that perhaps they actually feed you.

Of course, even in France, you can choose the wrong restaurant. I remember a painful, though not unfunny scene some years ago in a highly recommended establishment in the Auvergne. It was one of those maddening places which conform to convention by putting an attractively cheap but not fascinating menu outside the door. In such instances the hope of the owner is that you'll just regard this as a formality and be happy to pay at least three times as much: the price of the next menu on the upwards scale.

Not wishing to fork out a small fortune and having a long

drive ahead of me on a warm afternoon, I asked for the basic menu as advertised outside (it wasn't even shown to me at table), and was rewarded with a look of incredulity not unmixed with loathing. The waiter positively stamped away to the kitchen and I could well imagine the words 'Perfidious Albion' echoing through the steamy air there.

Just how basic that make-believe menu was I can demonstrate by the fact that the main course was omelette. Now I don't decry omelettes, especially the French variety. And the French do reckon they can make a better omelette than anyone on earth. (I dispute this: the champion of all omelette cooks, in my experience, is my own wife.) Nevertheless, in theory you'll get a much better omelette in the Auvergne than you'll ever hope for in Scunthorpe.

But however skilled the cook, if he or she is filled at the time with chagrin and irritation, a botch will be made of the dish. And especially if the moronic customer is deemed unworthy of professional attention.

What was banged down in front of me was an omelette which had gone very wrong indeed. In fact it looked positively scrambled. 'Unacceptable, I'm afraid,' I said. The waiter paled with fury; there was a gasp from surrounding tables where people were tucking into lobster, foie gras, soufflé, and other French pleasures.

I munched a piece of bread and did my best to look unconcerned. The waiter marched off again, to return a few minutes later with an even nastier travesty of the real thing – made worse by its being too greasy and covered with bits of burnt fat. 'No way,' I said.

The air around me was positively charged with electricity now. Everyone stopped eating. The waiter said tensely: '*Madame* is famous throughout Auvergne for her omelettes.'

'Then let her make me one,' I replied.

'*Monsieur*, this is a good omelette.'

'Bring the *patron*,' I demanded.

'He is busy with his accounts.'

'If Mohammed won't go to the mountain . . . ' I said. Picking up my omelette plate, I headed for the foyer.

Monsieur, who must have known just what was going on,

bent studiously over his account books as I strode up to him. I thrust the offending dish under his nose. 'I'm informed that this is what you call an omelette,' I said. 'I must beg to differ with you.'

He reached out a languid hand, forked the omelette from the plate, thrust his nose at it, sniffed, dropped the floppy thing back on the plate with a squelching noise and asked coldly: 'What is wrong with it?'

I didn't get a chance to reply, for the enemy had suddenly become reinforced. The kitchen door flew open, letting out a cloud of steam, an enraged *madame*, her equally enraged mother, two burly sons and my favourite waiter. I began to feel like Wellington would have felt if Waterloo had gone the other way.

They surrounded that wretched omelette, they poked at it, they picked it up and waved it in the air. 'Never before, *monsieur*,' *madame* shrilled, 'have we had complaints about our omelettes. They are famous throughout the *département*. And you have made my mother miss her bus to Clermont Ferrand with all this fuss.'

'Well, I'm not paying for that damned omelette,' I said.

'I did not hear *monsieur* correctly,' the *patron* rumbled.

'Oh yes you did,' I said. 'I'm only paying for what I had . . . even the bread if you like.' (At this he gave me a pitying smile.)

'How much for a pichet, a quarter of a tomato, and two little pieces of sausage?' I persisted.

He leered in triumph. 'As *monsieur* ordered the whole menu, he must pay the fixed sum.' The whole family screamed their approval.

Suddenly I was tired of him and his family, his dratted restaurant, his appalling omelette. My appetite had vanished. Resignedly I paid the menu price. Wellington had lost after all. But Perfidious Albion was determined to show *savoir faire*, even in adversity.

I turned to *grand-mère*. '*Madame*,' I said politely, 'can I give you a lift into Clermont Ferrand?'

The gesture availed me nothing – she came.

It's not the fault of the Portuguese hire-car industry that I'm still alive today. I've sat transfixed watching our rear wheel *overtake* the car while my driver veered desperately towards a grassy bank to bring us to rest tilted in a shower of sparks. On a day of torrential rain in Estoril – and I've never known rain wetter than the Portuguese variety outside an Eastern monsoon – driving with my windows up, I suddenly felt about to choke and unable to swallow. Exhaust fumes were leaking through the floor. I drove grimly on to the nearest garage, windows down, rain in my face. Better wet than dead . . .

Once in my early days of travel writing, when I occasionally journeyed with colleagues, our chauffeur was driving too fast downhill at Sagres to turn at a T-junction. We shot across the road, up a steep bank on the other side – and took off.

There wasn't even time for scenes of my past life to flash before my eyes; but at least I knew for a couple of terrifying seconds what it must be like to feel you had no chance of survival. For the cliffs of Sagres and Cape St Vincent are hundreds of feet high.

But we were still a few yards from the edge when we came to rest with a thump in long grass – miraculously on all four wheels. I was thrown violently against the roof, bruising my back and shoulders. The chap next to me in the back seat was trapped by his clothing when his door caved in, and the unfortunate journalist in front hit his head a terrible whack on the windscreen and dashboard.

And the culprit? He was completely unscathed. He leapt out of the car, cast an anguished look at us all, sat down on the ground and burst into tears. The car engine was still running. It was turned off, as I remember, by one of the farm workers who rushed to extricate us.

We had to take our injured colleague to a clinic to have his bleeding head dressed. We had words with the police, asking them to let the rest of the party at Faro know we'd be late for dinner, and then hired a taxi. And we arrived at Faro in time to stop them telephoning our respective offices that we had gone over the cliff and presumably were all dead. Somehow, the message had become garbled . . .

But I have a weakness, a special affection, for the Portuguese and I forgive them everything, even their hire cars, even their dreadful green soup that looks and tastes like it's made of seaweed and cabbage water, their unspeakable dried cod and their cloying, over-rich eggy puddings that stick to the roof of your mouth and give you an atrocious thirst. Any nation that has reason to call itself our oldest ally, which still venerates my own hero Wellington so long after he drove the French out, is OK by me. Portugal is a lovely little country, too, especially the lush green north.

And, more especially, the Azores, to my mind their most underrated tourist gem.

Not that my first experience of those tiny islands far out in the Atlantic gave me any inkling that one day I would start a long love affair with them. At that time, if you wanted to fly to the most interesting of the group, Sao Miguel, you flew from Lisbon to the least interesting, Santa Maria, and changed to a smaller plane for the last leg. But the Atlantic blew a gale and went on blowing it for days. I was trapped there with a lot of other discontented types under the tin roof of the airport hotel. Each day I would walk the few yards to the departure hall, huddled against the wind and rain, only to be told with a shrug: '*Senhor* – sorry. Maybe the plane come today, maybe not – I think maybe not.'

And each day I would return morosely to a lunch that consisted of the inevitable green soup, something schnitzelly and fresh pineapple – the latter (also served at each dinner) the proudest product of Sao Miguel, an island I was not fated to see on that trip. In fact, after a couple of days on Santa Maria, I had decided that my best plan was to get the first flight back to the mainland and abandon the whole idea of a feature on the Azores until a better season. There was the chance, I was told, that the little inter-island plane might get off one day, but being stranded on Sao Miguel, then not equipped for long-range flights, could be even worse. (Although had I known then what I know now about Sao Miguel – that it is one of the most beautiful places on earth – I might not have minded taking a chance of being marooned.)

The ants which infested the airport hotel added to my determination to quit the Azores at the first opportunity. Each morning I would awake to find them marching in strict military formation into my sponge bag. Each day I would complain to the management, who would spray the room. And each day following, the Panzers would be back and they would penetrate that bag, even when it was zipped up. I never could work out what they found so attractive in there. They showed no interest in my other possessions, and even when in despair I emptied out the wretched bag, they still marched inside.

At long last came deliverance: an American jet battled its way down through the wind. What seemed like half the population of the Azores crammed into it with me – for its next stop was Boston and the majority of my fellow-passengers were Azoreans heading for a new life in the New World. It was hardly the shortest way home for me, but anything was better than eating schnitzel and rapidly palling pineapple and coping with the airport-hotel ants.

That flight was not the most comfortable of my many trans-Atlantic crossings. The plane seemed to take an eternity to get above the storm; most of the migrants had not flown before and were not only emotionally upset at leaving home, but upset in a different way when trying to tackle the rich American meal. The result was sheer chaos.

'Do-you-speak-English, sir?' a stewardess screamed at me above the hubbub of sobbing children and gulping, retching adults.

'Yes,' I said.

'Thank Gahd. Would-you-please-explain-to-your-fellow-countrymen – '

'Hang on,' I said. 'I'm afraid I don't speak Portuguese.'

'Oh my Gahd!'

When I next saw the Azores conditions were happily different. Now I was due to visit all nine of them – under clear blue skies and on a calm sea. I was to see them at their best: brilliant with huge blue hydrangeas, matching the gorgeous colours of the lakes deep in craters of long-extinct volcanoes. See them when their tiny old windmills stood sharply etched on the horizon and I could fill my lungs with clear Atlantic air as I climbed dramatic headlands. My wife and I were passengers aboard a venerable cargo liner which in those days was the outer islands' only link with mainland Portugal.

The passenger accommodation was crummy to say the least – I had to fight to prevent my wife being whisked off to a sort of women's dormitory while I was to be bedded down with the males. Somehow or other, we managed to get a cabin to ourselves.

But there were no other snags aboard. I shall remember that voyage always. We sailed at night and tied up at each island all day and were taken ashore – in tenders to islands too small for a quay or simply down the rickety gangway at those big enough for us to go alongside. And all day, while we explored those delightful little spots then barely touched by tourism, the crew were busy loading and unloading everything from cows to huge reels of cable wire and the inevitable pineapples.

Somehow they seldom seemed to have completed the operation by the time we were back for dinner. And they'd still be loading cows aboard in slings and stowing them in the hold when the captain, immaculate in white dress uniform, would lead my wife on to the dance floor to open the evening festivities.

Somehow, too, the word had got around that there was a British journalist and his wife among the passengers – an event so rare, it seemed, as to warrant not only headlines in the local island papers, but to be the lead item on the Azores radio network we listened to aboard: '*Senhor* De Fries and his *esposa* will today be arriving in Flores.' I'd never had such large-scale personal publicity before.

Senhor De Fries and his *esposa*, welcomed in tiny Flores with all the formalities accorded to a visiting Cabinet Minister, were whisked off on a tour in an elderly car driven by a young man keenly aware of his responsibilities and apparently threatened with a terrible fate if he failed to deliver us back to the ship in time for sailing: she wouldn't be calling there again for another month.

Inevitably, as with so many other Portuguese cars in which I have driven, the wretched thing broke down in the middle of nowhere. The young man was plainly on the verge of breaking

43

into sobs of an intensity to match those of my driver who nearly had us all over the Sagres cliffs back on the mainland, when a mini-bus filled with cheerful fellow-passengers drew up.

They were islanders working in Lisbon and on their annual visit home. They were off to a picnic, and by forcing two wailing tots to perch themselves precariously on the back-window ledge, they managed to squeeze us in. 'No worry,' they assured us. 'We have plenty food for you – we eat, drink, then go back to the ship.'

But there was going to be precious little feasting for *Senhor* and *Senhora* De Fries that day on Flores. For it transpired that the spot our hosts had chosen – the very place, they told us, that they picked each year – was beyond a noticeboard adorned with skull and crossbones and the chilling message: 'Danger of death'.

We looked at each other appalled. We were even more appalled when the next sight to greet us around a bend in the road was a massive wire fence overlooked by watchtowers and guarding a series of dalek-like contraptions and metal humps from which arose a sinister humming. The gates, fantastic as it may sound, proved to be unlocked – they just pushed open.

Into this James Bond setting bumped the mini-bus, passing through shadows cast by the deserted watchtowers. The gates at the far end, through which we made our exit, were also unlocked.

High on a rearing clifftop, a few yards from the boundaries of what turned out to be an American nuclear establishment of a highly secret variety, we stopped with a jerk and everyone clambered out. The mites on the back ledge stopped crying at the sight of the food and soft drinks being unloaded and our hosts were so delighted with themselves and their surroundings that I wondered desperately how to tell them that I really wasn't all that hungry. My appetite had gone, my mouth had dried up and I couldn't take my eyes off that ominous-looking enclosure.

It was a struggle for both *Senhor* and his *esposa* to eat and drink, but we exchanged looks which clearly meant that we would both have to try to avoid giving offence. It was also a struggle to ask, in the merry din they all made, the two most obvious questions: 'Why picnic here?' and 'Where are the guards?' The answers, when we got them, were typically Portuguese – and frankly warranted no further discussion.

'We are here, *senhor*, because we have come here for years: long before this nuclear station was built. And why no guards? Because, *senhor*, it is Sunday. Have some more beer, *senhor*.'

Corvo is the tiniest of the Azores, a mere volcanic peak sticking dramatically out of the Atlantic with a minute village at the water's edge. I doubt whether even today it boasts more than its one old car, minus glass, the proud possession of the Mayoress. That car groaned and rattled us up the solitary road to a point where it could climb no higher. Then, guided by a youngster on leave from the distant University of Lisbon and chosen for his English, we scrambled up the mountain path to see Corvo's one tourist attraction: the crater itself.

On this expedition we were joined by a fellow-passenger from Lisbon, a large, jovial Portuguese history professor who was, as I remember, busy researching the life of Columbus. But his joviality wore thin when a cloud suddenly descended and our guide lost his path back to the village.

You didn't need a word of Portuguese to guess what he was roaring at the stricken student as we scrambled down through the damp, clinging mist, knocking ourselves against suddenly looming rough stone walls and dislodging stones from them. The large professor was even less designed than myself for climbing over walls we could barely see. But despite the discomfort and the nagging thought that soon it would be dark and the ship would sail without us and leave us stranded for a month, I found myself helpless with laughter. My wife, too, was fighting for self-control. The madder the professor got with the hapless guide: 'How can it be possible, imbecile, to lose your way on your own little island where there's only one path?', the more ludicrous the situation seemed to be.

'There's only one way to go,' I heard myself saying, 'and that's down, and we are going down, aren't we?' Then, suddenly, things did not seem quite so funny. I was sobered by the thought that we might find ourselves going over a sheer drop into the sea at any moment.

Just as suddenly, the professor stumbled, fell, and stayed down, puffed out. 'A moment, *senhor*, to get my breath.' The student stood wringing his hands and gazing at him in misery. His despair spread to us all. We could do right now with a navigator as sure as the professor's hero, I thought.

Then, out of the mist, like an apparition from another world, came rescue: a tall bearded shaggy cowherd, complete with staff, a sort of woolly jerkin, with crossed thonged leggings of cowhide and wearing rough sandals. He looked straight out of the Old Testament. He helped the professor to his feet and we followed him wordlessly towards the sea, with him striding ahead of us sure-footed on the steep slope, avoiding obstacles with all the experience of a lifetime of tending his cows on tiny Corvo.

And there were the huddled cottages of the village ahead of us. There were the tiny stone landing-place, the waiting boat, and through the thinning mist, the dim outline of our old ship.

I fished in my pocket, found escudo notes and coins, tried to press them into our rescuer's hand. But stern-faced, he shook his head violently. Then, without a word, he strode back up the mountainside, vanishing so quickly into the cloud that it was almost as if I had imagined him.

If pressed, I would describe Italians as on the whole better, surer drivers than the Portuguese. Not that I haven't been a terrified car passenger on Italian roads in my time. I never think of Sicily, for example, without the hair-raising memory of the taxi-driver who once took me down a one-way road tunnel – in the wrong direction. Halfway through, headlights blazed in our faces: an enormous truck was roaring towards us. We stopped so fiercely that I nearly fell through the windscreen. The truck, thank heaven, had good brakes, too. And stopped within inches of us. I don't think I've ever been more frightened.

For what seemed an eternity the taxi-driver and I stared numbly at the furious face of the man behind the lorry wheel. Then, as he reached for the door handle, obviously to get out and give my driver richly deserved hell, the latter recovered his nerve, slammed us into reverse and we went hurtling backwards to daylight and safety.

There was absolutely nothing I could say. And the driver was so overwhelmed by what he had done that he was speechless too. We found the right tunnel and plunged into it in grim silence. 'No,' I said later, in reply to his timid query, 'I'm not hungry for lunch; keep on going.' Imagine depriving an Italian – particularly a Sicilian – of his sacred long-drawn-out lunch! No breed of Italians is more argumentative and obstructive. But this Sicilian on this particular day just could not bring himself to protest.

That was, I suppose, about the only Italian misadventure I cannot look back on without at least a rueful grin. Italy – and I say it without disrespect to my many friends at the Italian State Tourist Office in London – has in itself all the makings of a mad comedy: it gets funnier, more muddled and confused, the further south you go.

Where else but at Catania, for example, would an Alitalia pilot, grabbed by me as he bustled from the flight deck, and asked to explain in English why we were stuck on the apron, strapped in our seats, reply with a shrug: 'Because-a she wont-a start!'

Where else but in Calabria, mainland Italy's deepest south, would two tourist offices refuse to collaborate on my behalf because the cities they represented were fighting each other for recognition as the regional capital?

And where else – again in Calabria – would a driver stop on a steeply sloping ravine bridge, persuade me to get out while he threw his arms into the air to emphasize the glorious view and be so daft as to leave off the handbrake? Out of the corner of my eye I saw the worst happening: the car, complete with my bags, passport, money, the lot, was rolling backwards to destruction.

With a wild yell I flung myself at it, was dragged along while reaching for the handbrake and somehow brought it to standstill. I rose, covered in dirt, to meet the eye of my escort. He was still standing with his arms raised in worship at the scenery, and surprise was just beginning to show on his face. 'Mamma mia!' he said, inevitably. 'I must have-a forgotten to-a putta ona da handbrake!'

'Oh?' I replied, between my teeth. 'So that was the cause of the trouble.'

Of course mad, very Italian situations occur well to the north of Rome, too. The Alitalia plane from London to Pisa was still short of the Alps when an appalling-looking creature, all legs and hairy feelers, was revealed to my startled gaze when I turned over the miserable scrap of meat served for lunch.

I summoned the stewardess. She stared at the insect, gave an operatic-type scream and seemed rooted to the spot. 'Take this tray away,' I said, 'and give me another.' She took the tray, but no replacement appeared. In the meantime everyone else was served, the coffee was brought, the trolley of duty-frees made its appearance – it must be an awful nuisance for airlines to have to serve food when there are those profitable goodies ready to be sold. But still no lunch for me.

I pressed the bell. *'Signore?'*

'Where's my lunch?' I demanded.

'Ah,' she said brightly. 'The gentleman with the beetle.'

'I sincerely hope I'm not still the gentleman with the beetle,' I told her. 'So where's my lunch?'

'We have-a no-a new lunch, *signore*. Da plane it is-a full up – no-a spares.'

'So if I had not asked you here and now for lunch I just would not have been given anything?' I said, incredulous.

She smiled. 'So sorry, *signore*.'

'This is a scheduled flight and you're supposed to feed me,' I said.

'But not when-a we don't have any left, *signore*!'

The chief steward was summoned – a typical Alitalia chief steward looking like an actor playing an admiral in a musical comedy but about to break into *Rigoletto* at any moment. 'So sorry, *signore*. But quite impossible to give you lunch.'

'Has the crew had lunch yet?' I asked.

'No, *signore*, but – '

'Lunch, please,' I insisted. 'You don't have to take someone's whole lunch away – you can surely make up a tray with bits and pieces from several trays. Just so long as you don't bring my own tray back here – with or without the insect.'

The admiral's eyes bulged, narrowed speculatively, widened

again. A thoughtful frown creased his serene Mediterranean countenance. He shrugged, muttered something to the stewardess and she proceeded to serve me the best lunch I've ever eaten on Alitalia or I suspect, will ever be likely to eat again. And I had metal knives and forks instead of plastic.

Sensation among the passengers. 'Here, look what he's got! How did you get that then?'

I smiled smugly. 'I'm travelling crew-class,' I told them. 'A lot of annoyance first, but it's worth it.'

But it is down south that it really all happens. And you can't get much further south than Pantelleria. During the Second World War this tiny island just off the Tunisian coast was a Mussolini naval fortress. Its peacetime potential began to be exploited without too much regard for all the concrete Musso left behind, a fair proportion of which seemed to have been poured into a barracks building eventually transformed into a third-class hotel. This sombre establishment was, unfortunately for me, the only place open on the island during an ill-advised winter visit.

I say 'ill-advised' because, as I was to learn to my cost, no one in his senses goes to Pantelleria until spring is really under way. I fear I must have fallen for all the rubbish about the place being a perpetual sun-trap, catching the warmth from nearby Africa and so on.

Now there isn't the slightest doubt that had anyone wished to dig up the past, to find out just how Mussolini's navy lived – and apparently co-operated in a most uncharacteristic way with Hitler's spartan 'strength-through-joy' programme – there was no better spot to choose than that hotel. It was not what you would call ship-shape; but the jets from the shower, although marked hot, were suitably icy – and when the supply had a fit of temperament and ran dry, the water was replaced by flakes of rust. So there was always something happening: you couldn't complain to the management – assuming that they understood more than a couple of words you said – that nothing was coming

49

out of the shower. All floors, needless to say, were solid concrete.

The menu was equally fascinating: constant cous-cous to remind you of the nearness of North Africa, spaghetti and some sort of lukewarm liquid alleged to be soup, but more like a rendered-down version of the green cabbage water they serve in Portugal. I was obliged to go into the question of meals at that particular hotel in some detail because there was not much choice of places to eat in the closed season.

At the end of my stay there, I was plainly the world's leading authority on the shore life of Mussolini's sailors – except of course for any experience they might have had in dubious establishments on the harbourside. I can only assume that these, unlike my hotel, had not survived Allied bombing. (You'd have needed an atom bomb at the very least to have more than dented that place.)

And my stay on that idyllic island was in fact longer than I had planned for the same dreary reason that I was obliged to get to know Santa Maria in the Azores – the weather turned nasty and the planes didn't come. And as with Santa Maria, I had enough time on my hands to explore every inch of Pantelleria. But if there were ever grounds for me to think: 'Come back Santa Maria, all is forgiven' then it was Pantelleria that provided them. Even the ants would have been a diversion. And on Santa Maria there were at least a number of other people in the same predicament as myself; we could console each other over the schnitzel and pineapple. On Pantelleria – a very simple but pleasant enough little place in good weather, I should imagine – there were only the natives, who thought I was mad to be there anyway.

The wretched island even ruined for me a suitably melancholy Beatles number I was stuck on at the time: 'Yesterday . . . all my troubles seemed so far away.' You could say that again, I thought. There's never a time when I hear that tune now that the memory of those six days on Pantelleria doesn't come flooding back. Sometimes I have dreamed I am still there and I wake up in a sweat. Six days? It was more like six months.

I haven't the faintest doubt that the island has now improved out of all recognition – with new hotels and what have you.

After all, I'm going back some years. I don't doubt, too, that if I hadn't been so crazy as to go there in winter, I would have formed a quite different opinion – so if by some wild chance you're thinking of going to Pantelleria this year, don't let me put you off. But, unfair though it sounds, I declare that I'd rather get a job digging holes in the road than go back to Pantelleria again. I'd read all the books I'd brought with me, I'd been around the island umpteen times and I thought that if they served me cous-cous again I'd go out of my mind.

On the sixth morning my nerve snapped. No plane coming? 'I fear not, *signore*.' I went to the apology of a post office and sent the following telegram to my wife: 'NIGHTMARE DIS-ORIENTATION VITAL ACKNOWLEDGE SAVE SAN-ITY.' I was still living near the dreaded Leatherhead, so you can imagine how long it took me to get the message understood and handled.

I'd hardly embarked on yet another plate of fascinating lunchtime spaghetti when the phone rang. 'Your plane it comes, *signore!*' cried the hotelier, who was probably as anxious to see the last of my forlorn face as I was to leave. It does the reputation of a former naval barracks very little good to have a discontented guest.

Clutching a ticket which was meant to get me home on the same day via Naples and Rome, I climbed joyfully aboard. 'My troubles *seem* so far away,' I sang happily to myself. There was Trapani ahead and the big, comforting shore of Sicily. Land, masses of land. Marvellous!

And then an eagle flew into one of the engines and they spent so long taking the tangled flesh and feathers out of the works at Trapani that I missed my Naples connection and eventually reached Rome five minutes after the last London plane had gone . . .

I telephoned my wife. 'Did you get my telegram?' I asked her.

'What telegram?'

'I sent it this morning. Still, never mind; it's out of date now,' I said. 'See you tomorrow.'

She still hadn't got that telegram from Pantelleria when I arrived home for lunch next day. But she wasn't kept in

51

suspense for much longer. It was delivered as we were finishing coffee and I was still getting the horrors of the last few days off my chest.

And there, in the heart of safe, sane, uncomplicated Surrey she read out solemnly: 'NIGHTMARE DISORIENTATION VITAL ACKNOWLEDGE SAVE SANITY.'

'Sounds like someone's in trouble somewhere,' she said.

'Well, it's certainly not me,' I told her.

But that long-delayed telegram wasn't Surrey's only reminder of life on an Italian island paradise. Lipari makes wine, grows capers and looks out on its volcanic little sisters, Stromboli and Vulcano. The local tourist office, to thank me for giving their domain publicity, once sent me a hefty box which I was later to discover contained a tiny keg of wine strong enough to render an entire family unconscious for most of one Christmas Day after two glasses per head (and I speak from personal experience); enough capers to satisfy a two-year demand from about half the Italian and French restaurants in Soho; some volcanic stones of odd shape and colour – and a lot of ash, presumably as padding for the rest of the contents.

The box arrived at my office; the contents list as specified in the attached Customs declaration was unreadable, and I decided that, as my wife loves surprises, I would take it home unopened and speculate with her as to what it contained before we delved inside.

What disturbed me, however, was the little deposit of mysterious grey powder it left on my desk top, and the trickle of the stuff from a tiny split that marked my passage to the office lift, into and across Fleet Street, on the Waterloo bus in the rush hour and on to my train. What could it be? I hoisted the box on to the luggage rack with a huge effort and sat down on the seat facing it.

A City type climbed aboard, and settled down on the seat directly under the box, unfolded his *Times* and began to read. I tried to read, too, but I couldn't take my eyes off the slowly growing pyramid of grey powder beginning to form on top of his bowler. I wanted to say something, but could not bring myself to utter a word. I was aware, too, that other eyes were being raised over the tops of newspapers. But – as you would expect in a commuter train – British politeness and a total lack of interest in one's neighbour held sway. And the gentleman, all unknowing, remained immersed in his newspaper while the evidence of a volcanic eruption in the far-off Mediterranean continued to settle on his bowler through Clapham Junction, Wimbledon and Raynes Park.

At Surbiton, still blissfully unaware that he was a marked man, he got out, complete with volcanic pyramid.

I'd love to think that he was an analytical chemist and was dumbfounded by what he discovered on his hat when he reached home. Or, how, if the stuff was recognized eventually for what it was, he was able to convince his wife that he hadn't taken a quick trip to the Med on a day he was supposed to be in Threadneedle Street.

3

FAR NORTH NEGATIVES
Sweden, Norway and Finland

People – and there seem to be no end of them – who think a travel writer's life is one long holiday, forget two important points. Firstly, unlike a real holidaymaker, he has to show the results of his going abroad at someone else's expense. Secondly, he is in theory at the beck and call of his office to cover any important news story that might break on the spot, and to answer any queries from the editor that may arise on his copy about to be run in the paper in his absence.

Obviously, if a writer tries to vary his contributions as widely as possible, he can be called upon to answer questions about one country while half a world away from it on another assignment when the call from London reaches him. Thus I have been asked to rack my brains about Scandinavian technicalties – how to spell the name of a particular dish and so on – while on a bad line in blazing heat in a Sahara hotel. And, on another occasion, in complete reverse, I have been quizzed about a Moroccan feast I attended weeks before I boarded a tramp steamer out of Hull for my next – and current – assignment: a long trip around the Norwegian fiords.

It was deep in the fiords that the office caught up with me. I lost count of the number of times that solemn Viking character – the shipping company's local agent – in long raincoat and soft hat would climb the ladder from a small boat and inform me that my office had phoned the previous day and would I please ring them at once. 'Someding about Africa, I think,' he would say, looking at me in a puzzled way.

From tiny fiord fishing village after tiny fiord fishing village I would endeavour to contact London – usually the ship docked too late in the day for me to catch anyone in my office, so it meant I would have to wait until the next stop. I grew to dread the appearance of those little boats on rainy evenings as we slowed to tie up at yet another village and publication day grew nearer.

Once, congratulating myself that I had finally been landed early enough to settle the outstanding queries before my office closed for the night, I found that the only telephone available was not working. Someone suggested that I tried the phones on the Norwegian side of the nearby frontier bridge with Sweden. I was driven there – but about two dozen brawny lorry-drivers were queueing to use the one phone and they were plainly in no mood to let a non-Viking get in first.

So there was nothing for it but to walk into Sweden and try to phone from there. With no disrepect to my Norwegian friends, my experience highlighted the difference between the Norwegian and Swedish ways of life: at the Swedish border control point I had the choice of no fewer than eight telephones.

'Where are you speaking from?' came a Caledonian rasp from London. 'Sweden? For God's sake what are you doing there?'

'Phoning you.'

'I thought you were in Norway. We've been trying to get you all over the damned country.'

'I couldn't phone from Norway, so I've gone into Sweden.'

'We didn't know you were going near Sweden!'

'Sweden happens to be next door to Norway,' I said. 'They have phones here.'

'Oh? Well, this is what we want to know . . . '

I always associate the far-north world with searching for something: explorers bound for the Pole, for a passage to Cathay. And myself searching for telephones, for reindeer, for the Russian border – and for the Swedish traditional Thursday meal of pea soup and pancakes.

I found the phone, as I have explained, even though it meant crossing the international frontier. The reindeer eluded me. I was up in Norway's northern territory, heading for the North

Cape and the Arctic Sea, and the only reindeer I had spotted for the whole trip hitherto had been one stuffed specimen, distinctly moth-eaten, outside a gift shop in Tromsö.

'How the devil,' I thought irritably, 'can I go home and not say I've seen reindeer?' (I'm a stickler for truth: I don't write about anything I haven't set eyes on. If I did, the chances are that I would get angry letters saying that whatever it was had been laid on for me by the tourist office, or I was a liar, because they – the letter-writers – had spent the earth following my suggested holiday programme and they were damned if they had seen anything like I said I saw.)

The days passed and those reindeer continued to elude me. There were wiry Lapps who assured me by sign language and without moving a muscle of their faces that the antlered horde had passed only hours before; there were huge bridge and ferry attendants who swore that no fewer than 300 reindeer had swum across before their very eyes that very morning. At Hammerfest, the northernmost city of all, the very mention of reindeer was enough to cause apoplexy. 'Always they come on the rampage, through the very streets, and the damage they can do . . . '

But no matter how many miles I travelled across the bleak tundra – right in fact to the very tip of North Cape itself, when I couldn't see a hand in front of me for swirling snow and sea-mist – there was not a sound or sight of reindeer. I was forced to the conclusion that my quarry had only one place to hide themselves – in the Arctic Sea itself. Plainly they had plunged, one by one, into the depths from North Cape, like outsize lemmings. Anything to escape publicity.

Now for all the fact that the North has wide-open spaces and little population, a desire to keep oneself to oneself is not necessarily a Scandinavian characteristic. In fact, if the Swedes are to be taken as an example, they are among the most publicity-conscious people on earth. Every town, however small, seems to have a proliferation of daily newspapers which have to be filled, however trivial the subject.

I was once on the Baltic island of Gotland. Fog set in within minutes of my landing from Stockholm; I could not see across Visby's main street. But waiting at my hotel, eager in pursuit of news to fill those hungry columns between the adverts, was a young female reporter, laden with camera equipment, pencils and notebooks. 'Please, Mr De Fries, tell me your impressions of our island.'

'How can I?' I said helplessly. 'I can't see through the fog and I've only just arrived. Can't you give me until tomorrow at least?'

'Tomorrow will be too late,' she told me. 'My rivals will be after you then.'

'But this is not fair,' I protested.

She considered the point. 'Well, I suppose we could do it like this. You come across to that souvenir shop there, let me take a picture of you buying a gift for your wife, and then I'll write a little story quoting you saying you are looking forward to seeing Gotland. That would mean I have my scoop.'

' "Looking forward to seeing Gotland when the fog clears," ' I suggested.

She winced. 'No – just looking forward to seeing Gotland. No mention of fog.'

'But everyone here must know about the fog today, surely. It's not running the place down to admit it.'

However, argument was in vain. Next morning, all over the front page, was a hideously large photograph of myself, almost life-size I swear, my coat collar turned up against the chill, posing with some Viking warrior toys and with me gushing in the caption space – there wasn't much room left after they printed the photograph and the paper's title – about how I was looking forward eagerly to seeing the island. I suppose, taking the words literally, that the sentiment was true enough. With a bit of luck, I'd actually *see* Gotland next day. I did – and very pleasant it was.

The Swedish passion for maximum press exposure has a bearing on my search for the Thursday meal of pea soup and pancakes. I'd taken my wife on her first Swedish trip and we looked in vain for this dish I'd written about on previous visits – Jennifer had thought it sounded attractive and she wanted to sample it.

It wasn't to be found anywhere that Thursday in Gothenburg: we were there at the wrong time of year. Pea soup and pancakes are deemed too heavy for summer. 'I still fancy it,' Jennifer said. 'Someone must serve it somewhere in a city this size. I challenge you to find it – and not have it laid on just for us, either.'

While she shopped I made a furtive visit to the tourist office. They arranged for me to 'find' pea soup and pancakes in a little cafeteria.

I took Jennifer there that night, assuring her poker-faced that I had discovered the dish on the menu myself. We were eating away happily when the door opened and in strode a reporter and photographer from one of the local dailies.

'Mr De Fries? The tourist office told us we'd find you here and they had arranged for you to have our winter Thursday meal.' I avoided Jennifer's smouldering eye and endeavoured to look casual and welcoming.

'May we have a photograph, please? My, pea soup and pancakes at this time of year! This must be a record.'

The photographer clicked away and the reporter asked Jennifer: 'Mrs De Fries, do you like this dish of ours?'

'Yes, thanks,' Jennifer replied tersely.

But that was not the end of our pea-soup- and pancake-eating in Gothenburg on that out-of-winter-season Thursday evening. To our dismay – replete as we were and now fully understanding why such a dish was not eaten in summer – the hotel had also heard of our search for this so-special Swedish delicacy. The manager greeted us with a proud smile. 'Just for you,' he said, 'we have prepared pea soup and pancakes – real Swedish-winter-style.'

Our hearts sank, but we flashed warning looks at each other not to reveal our feelings. There was no escape, no alternative to sitting down without a scrap of appetite left and eating a second dinner, identical with the first. And, like the first, the helpings were enormous . . .

The tourist office kindly translated next day's press story for us. We had, it seemed, been searching vainly for years for this dish, but summer after summer we had been disappointed. Finally, due to the kindness of Mr Olsen, in co-operation with the city tourist authorities, it had been arranged specially, and here was a shot of the British couple tucking in with great heartiness. Mrs De Fries told the newspaper that she liked the food so much she was taking home the recipe to England where she hoped that it would eventually replace roast beef and Yorkshire pudding as the national dish.

'I wouldn't say anything so daft!' Jennifer exploded.

'It only goes to show,' I told her, 'that you can't believe a word you read in the papers.'

My search for the Russian frontier was, in one sense, successful. In another, it was almost a disaster. The long-closed Karelian border between the Soviet Union and Finland is the object of popular guided excursions from Helsinki and other Finnish tourist centres. What the tourist buses emphatically don't do is to take an ever-narrowing road through seemingly endless pine forests.

Along this road, becoming progressively rougher as the trees closed in, I was bumped along one day in a car driven by a young woman guide from Helsinki who, only when she had nearly caused us both to be involved in an international incident and facing arrest, admitted to me that her knowledge of the area was scanty.

'Are you sure we're on the right road?' I asked uneasily. 'Coaches couldn't even get along here.'

'This is the only road.'

'But now it's little more than a track. We couldn't even turn round.'

'This is the only road. You asked to see the border – I'm taking you to it.'

She stopped beside a tiny wooden hut near a railway track. 'I'll ask them to open the level-crossing pole so that we can drive on,' she said.

She walked across to the hut, knocked and went inside. The silence was shattered by a burst of angry voices. The hut door flew open and the guide came out fast and looking pale. Behind her strode a fur-hatted soldier, unslinging a sub machine-gun, his face furious.

He marched up to me, roared in English: 'What are you doing here? This area is closed to all foreigners. Didn't you see the sign twenty kilometres back?'

'I thought we were going to have a look at the Russian frontier,' I said limply.

'The frontier? What the devil to you think *this* is? Do you see him? He pointed a mittened hand across the railway line. In the distance, on the far side, was another hut. A Russian soldier was studying us through binoculars.

'Show me your passport,' the Finnish guard demanded. 'My God, a British journalist! This will cause trouble – on both sides. The Russians will complain . . . '

He snapped instructions in Finnish to the abashed guide. With difficulty she turned the car around and we drove off down the track.

'He said,' she reported sullenly, 'that he will telephone the first village along the way. We will be stopped there by the police and you'll have to make a statement.'

'So we *were* on the wrong road,' I said.

'It was the road to the frontier.'

'But not the road the coaches take,' I persisted.

'It was the road to the frontier.'

It transpired that of course there was more than one road to that long-closed frontier. The wide, approved road the coaches took, and the one we chose. No civilian, it seemed, had driven our road in years. Let alone a British travel writer, accompanied by a tourist guide who took a permanently lowered border pole to be a level-crossing barrier and coolly asked for it to be raised.

I was let off with a caution. I've been doubly cautious about frontiers ever since. And about guides who assure me they know the way.

I stood one day peering up at a towering Norwegian peak, reached by a barrel lift – individual open-topped barrels each holding two standing passengers. 'I don't like the look of that lift,' I said. 'Swaying all over the place. Twenty minutes up and twenty down. Not for me, thanks.'

'But for me though,' Jennifer said. We agreed I would drive to the mountain top and meet her there. She was whisked skywards and I headed for the road up. But just a short distance from the valley, I was forced to turn back; the road was blocked by a landslide.

Back at the barrel-lift office, I made an urgent request. Could they telephone their mates at the top and when a British lady – small, curly-haired, oh, about this height – arrived, send her straight down as her husband couldn't drive up to meet her. It all seemed so simple.

What I hadn't reckoned on was that I wasn't fully understood. Someone – either at the foot of the cableway or at the top – took my request to mean that any British person who arrived was to be pushed straight down again without being allowed to land. And unfortunately, behind Jennifer's barrel came twenty other barrels, each containing two members of a British mini-cruise party equipped with picnic lunch to be eaten on the mountain top as the highlight of a tightly scheduled, brief visit to western Norway.

The dire result was that Jennifer's descending barrel was followed closely by receptacles containing furious mini-cruisers who, as soon as they admitted to being British, had found their barrels being pushed heartily to the downwards cable. And down they went, their protests ignored, the mountainside echoing with bewildered shouts to their passing friends still heading upwards. 'They won't let you land!'

'Why not?'

'Dunno. They just say: "British go down." ' Adult shouts and juvenile wails went on for the whole length of the barrel cableway.

'What *have* you done?' Jennifer demanded, as the trippers, still clutching their picnic lunches, crowded around the bewildered guides, who appealed to the cableway officials. Who pointed in my direction. I flung open the car door. 'Get in for God's sake – I'll explain later,' I said. 'There's going to be a riot.'

And reporting a riot demands a particular journalistic technique – especially if you and yours are the unwitting cause of it.

So we fled.

4
SOARING AMONG THE ALPS
Austria, Switzerland and Italy

There's a pleasant little village on the banks of the fast-moving Inn near Innsbruck I took a fancy to years ago – such a strong fancy in fact that I started my piece on the Austrian Tyrol with a description of a chairlift descent from the mountain towering above it. There was a tonsil-stretching Teutonic rasp about the actual name of that mountain, but translated into English it could not have sounded more romantic: the Mountain of Midsummer Day.

That title captured the imagination of many *Sunday Express* readers on holiday in the Tyrol that summer and I continued to receive many inquiries about the village and its facilities well into the following year. It was some time before I found myself there again, and I was flattered to learn on arrival that the locals seemed to have remembered virtually every word I had written about their domain and had played host to a record number of British visitors arriving with a copy of my article and asking to be directed to the chairlift almost before they had unpacked.

My reward for helping to improve Anglo-Tyrolean relations was a slap-up lunch at the mountain's foot with the local tourist-office director. The weather was glorious, the mountain rose in majesty high above me, every detail of its massive formation clear and sharp in the clean air.

'*Ach, Herr* De Fries,' my host said. 'We are in your debt. But one thing puzzles us. Why when you mentioned the mountain did you leave out the most important detail about it?'

It was my turn to be puzzled. 'What do you mean?' I asked him.

'Look more closely, *Herr* De Fries. Can't you see what I mean? It is what you call standing out a mile, I think.'

I gazed at the mountain. 'Sorry,' I said. 'You baffle me.'

'My dear *Herr* De Fries,' he said, shaking his head wonderingly. 'And you such an observant man, too. Look very hard at that little ledge near the peak. Does it not seem like a lock of hair? Further down, that sharp piece of rock – the nose, *ja*? Further down still, another point – the moustache? And then the chin. See, there . . . A face, *Herr* De Fries. A famous face. For this and not the name our mountain is known. And this you did not write about.'

A lock of hair, a sharp nose, a moustache? Light reluctantly dawned. 'You wanted me to write about *Hitler's* face?' I asked in amazement.

'Why not?'

'You baffle *me*,' I said. 'You wish me to make up for that terrible lapse next time, then? So, I'll tell you what I will do, my dear sir. I'll call your mountain the Midsummer Hitler Mountain or the Mountain of Midsummer Hitler. How's that? Or perhaps you think it won't sound quite so romantic as the way we had it before. Personally, I think British visitors would love the change. They'll flock here in thousands, not hundreds.'

This was too much even for him. 'That is good joke, I think,' he said, looking at me uncertainly now. 'Perhaps it would be better to keep the name they know through your so-marvellous article. But I'm still surprised you did not notice Hitler's face up there the first time you came.'

'So am I, so am I,' I said. 'But then I suppose I don't go looking for it.'

I'm fed up with being told by tourist officials in mountain areas that virtually every lump of rock – whether on the heights or in some dank, slippery grotto – has a name, represents or resembles something or other. 'This is what we call Eagle Rock. Do you see the flying angel near the roof – up there, look. The baby – do you see the baby? And the lion about to spring? And doesn't that rock there remind you of Napoleon – the cocked hat, everything?

They're mad about that sort of sightseeing explanation in the Austrian Tyrol. On the same day that the Mountain of

Midsummer Hitler became an indispensable part of my reportage I was shown another great rock formation on the horizon and asked what I thought it resembled. I bit back an acid reply that it looked like Hermann Goering seated behind the controls of a Heinkel III and said, quite truthfully as it happened, that to me it seemed remarkably close to a woman working a typewriter.

Of course I was miles out. Presumably typewriters weren't invented when some idiot decided what that rock represented. I had no romantic streak in me, that was the trouble. 'My dear *Herr* De Fries. How could you! That is a mother with her baby! Our legends say she sinned and was turned to stone.'

I'm happy to tell you that I wasn't the only British Philistine roaming the Tyrol that day. In the handsome heart of Innsbruck is an impressive figure of a holy woman on a column. Above her head is a halo, seemingly made of metal and held on by a rod fastened to the back of the statue's neck. I was walking close to a coach-tour party from Yorkshire and couldn't help hearing the comments.

'Ooze that chap oop there, then? Ancient Roman he looks like froom 'ere. In toga?' We were approaching from the back at the time.

'That's a laurel wreath he's wearing or ah'm mooch mistaken. Julius Caesar, is it?'

I felt sorry for their guide. 'Pliss, pliss, walk to der front. Dat ist Saint Anna – not der chap!'

'By goom, sorry lad. I didn't see t'hoop.'

'HALO, HALO! Not der hoop,' the guide spluttered in despair.

I fled the scene. You can't take us anywhere.

I yield to no man in my love for the Italian Tyrol – Sud Tirol to its stubbornly German-speaking inhabitants, filled with sentimental longings to be part of Austria again; Alto Adige to its Italian rulers who must sometimes regret taking the place on when frontiers were redrawn after the First World War. The truth is of course that the South Tyroleans are about as Italian as I am.

I am besotted with the Dolomite scenery, with the rich mixture of two cuisines, by the splendid wine. But you can have strange encounters in the South Tyrol. You might find yourself, as I did, near Bolzano one day sharing a table at an open-air restaurant with a pleasant-faced young man who told me casually: 'My father he is a sort of Nazi. The Italians have him in prison now for planting bombs under a viaduct.'

'And are you a sort of Nazi, too?'

He shrugged. 'Not really. I don't go in for that sort of thing.'

'Do you agree with your father that the South Tyrol should go back to Austria?'

'Well,' – another shrug. 'A little late for that now, I think.'

'But do you consider yourself an Italian?'

'Good *Gott* no!'

There was also the day, again near Bolzano, when I lost my appetite in the middle of a delicious lunch. I was in one of those delightful little mountain inns, with all the sylvan beauty of the Dolomites around me. Dozens of carefree tourists of all nationalities relaxed in dazzling sunshine. It all seemed a million miles from anything ugly and sordid.

Then the massively built owner loomed over me, asked if I was British and what my job was. I told him I was writing a travel piece about the region and he beamed and sat down with me. 'What can I do to get more British customers?' he asked me.

'Go on serving good food like this,' I told him. 'There's no better recommendation than word of mouth, if you see what I mean.'

'I have more than food for them,' he said. 'I have a good story to tell. Very entertaining and interesting.' He beckoned to one of the waiters who a few minutes later handed me a folder. Inside were cuttings from British newspapers reviewing a book on the life of Mussolini. My host's name was mentioned several times; he was a senior officer of Himmler's SS and his duties in the last months of the war included keeping Mussolini's wife and mistress from each other's throats.

When I looked up from the file he had adorned the table with a photograph of himself in black-and-silver uniform, complete with death's-head symbol. He was smiling proudly. As, to use the terminology of certain tabloid contemporaries of the *Sunday Express*, I 'made an excuse and left', the smile faded and he seemed quite surprised. Even a little hurt.

Switzerland has a particular place in my affections. To snobs who say loftily that its scenery is 'predictable, all chocolate-box pretty-pretty' I can only reply: 'I'll have a lot more boxes, then. Swiss chocolates suit me very well.'

To me Swiss scenery is superb; the very variety offered and the tastefulness of presentation of restaurant dishes has an appeal all its own. Though I've yet to discover a foolproof method of keeping a duvet from falling off me during the night, the pure mountain air ensures this customary poor sleeper a good night's rest with the prospect of awakening next morning to that marvellous aroma of freshly brewed coffee and of croissants brought straight from the oven.

I even enjoy the Swiss businesslike approach in their dealings with people like me. I shall always treasure the questionnaire about what assistance I might need sent to me by the Swiss National Tourist Office in London after I told them I was planning a visit to the tiny principality of Liechtenstein, whose tourism they handle. Question No. 10 was: 'Tea with the royal family? Please answer yes or no.'

My reply to that was: 'Yes, if time.' This was plainly thought to be on the cool side, even by the eager-to-please Swiss. I did not get my tea and torte at Vaduz Castle. But I relished being asked.

The Swiss, you learn, are ready for anything – even for war. Those easy-on-the-eye chalets dotting green velvety slopes are most likely to be equipped with atomic shelters, and farmers bringing in plump cows for milking across meadows glowing with gentians keep military uniforms and sub machine-guns in their lofts.

'*Ach*, those Swiss,' grumbled the Leichtenstein official who greeted me on my first trip to the principality. 'Do you hear those guns booming across the valley? That is the Swiss Army. War, always war. They think of nothing else.'

But military preparedness apart, Switzerland is a great place for a holiday. They like the British, too, And so they should. After all, when it comes to tourism – both the summer and winter variety – who put them on the map? Their hoteliers are professional to the last degree; for all the warmth of their welcome they are businessmen.

I shall never forget quibbling over the steepness of the bill one little place high in the Bernese Oberland handed me on check-out. 'How can you justify charging so much for boiled eggs?' I demanded.

'Overheads, *Mein Herr*,' said the cashier.

'What overheads, for goodness sake? You even have your own chickens up here,' I protested.

'*Ja*, but the *adlers* – the eagles. They swoop down and steal the chickens. They are our overheads.'

As someone who files thousands of miles per year, I can't write about Switzerland without a word of praise for the airline which bears the Swiss red cross emblem. I've no interest to declare here except as a highly satisfied passenger; I've never occupied a free seat on Swissair and my company has always paid the full fare on my behalf. (You can always tell when travel writers have been on a freebie. Somewhere or other in their piece they'll talk of looking out of the window of their Air France, KLM, SAS, B Cal and so forth jet.)

Swissair are as efficient, as time-conscious, as reliable, as the Swiss themselves. And however 'Teutonic' their system seems to be in our eyes, they are never to my knowledge the targets of the sort of unkind stories which must make long-suffering Lufthansa officials throw up their hands in despair. You know what I mean: 'Ladies and gentlemen. Dis is Captain von Muller speaking. Ve haff just had engine failure and come down in der sea. Pliss do not panic. Dose who can svim pliss assemble mit your life jackets on der left ving of der aircraft. Dose who cannot svim, on der right ving. To dose on der left ving pliss be informed dat der shore ist just vun kilometre avay. On der beach you vill find a Lufthansa representative vaiting to deal mit all queries and to book your onvard connections. To dose on der right ving: thank you for flying Lufthansa.'

Swissair have saved my sanity on more than one occasion when I would otherwise have been stranded at some of my least favourite airports. The most recent instance was at Colombo, where, in the middle of a frantic mob sweltering out of reach of what air-conditioning was on tap – confined to the far side of the passport control to which we could not be admitted until the flight was called – I was horrified to learn that my eastbound plane from Europe would be eight hours late.

There was no point in trying to go back to the city to pass the time; I knew there wasn't a vacant hotel room to be had as an international conference was just starting. The heat was unbearable. And in that airport there wasn't even a comfortable chair in sight.

Despairingly I consulted the departures board. There was just one flight posted as about to take off for Singapore, my destination. Swissair. I forced my way through the throng, panted up to the desk, thrust my ticket into the Swiss official's hand and pleaded: 'Can you take me?'

For a moment he looked doubtful and my heart sank. Then he said: 'One business-class seat, sir? OK. But you must be quick.' I threw my suitcase on the scales, he spoke urgently on the telephone. Then: 'Just one thing, sir. A snag.' He looked grave and my heart sank.

'I am very sorry, sir. But we will not be able to give you a business-class meal.'

'Oh, God,' I said. 'Is that all? To hell with the meal. Just get me on the plane.'

When I was thankfully settling into my seat the official came up to me beaming. 'All OK sir. I have fixed it. You will have a business-class meal.' He looked as pleased and relieved as if he was having that meal himself.

The meal, as I was sure it would be, was beyond reproach. But I imagine that the tourist-class version could not have been far behind.

Then there was the rescue by Swissair early one morning of a dishevelled and demoralized De Fries at Istanbul. I had passed a grim night after missing my plane home; the only accommodation I could find was in a grubby motel which, judging by the night-long uproar outside, seemed to be just at the end of the main runway. Creepy-crawlies scuttled across the concrete floor; flaked rust, reminiscent of my being marooned in Pantelleria, spattered down when I tried the shower. To add to the noise of plane engines that kept me awake throughout the sweaty night was the guttural din of hearty German tourists of the Strength-through-Joy variety, sprawled at tables on the verandah under my window, their drinking songs punctuated by the crash of breaking glasses and bottles.

At first light next day, I paid a too-high bill and, unshaven – the electric plugs in my room hadn't worked and there was no hot water for a safety razor – I ignored the entreaties of red-eyed junkies who offered to carry my luggage in return for part of their air fare home to Britain. And I headed for the airport, determined to catch whatever flight was going westwards.

Only one plane was standing there in the cool light of early morning – Swissair. Have you ever wanted to kiss a jet liner? From its position I knew it must have come in the night before and therefore it had to be taking off early. And in the right direction for me. Yes, it was going to Zürich. Yes, the Swissair desk could book me on to London. There was one seat left out of Istanbul. Tourist-class. (This was before business travel caught up with Swissair, who held out against it for a long time, making the point that their tourist-class accommodation was at very least equal to every other European airline's business-class – a not unreasonable claim at the time and not far short of the position prevailing today.)

Climbing into that gently cooled, spotless aircraft was like mounting the steps to a different world. An electric shaver was produced, lots of hot water gushed from the taps. A blonde, blue-eyed, slender vision who would have gladdened the heart of any sex-starved William Tell gave me a glass of iced *fresh* orange juice; coffee beyond the wildest dreams of any passenger on virtually any other airline; freshly baked rolls and croissants that I prefer to believe had no connection whatever with any Istanbul bakery (although logic tells me they must have); black-cherry jam, unlimited creamy Swiss butter. And, to top it all, an omelette, light as air, cooked to perfection.

The grubbiness and squalor of that past night was a distant

memory in no time. Almost, it seemed, before that blonde vision whisked the breakfast tray away and gave me magazines and newspapers to read, the clouds parted to show soft green valleys nestling at the foot of snow-capped mountains. Physically, I was more than three-quarters of the way home. Mentally, I was already there.

Now you may say you can't understand why I attach such great store to these two instances of rescue by Swissair. Surely, any airline with a vacant seat just before take-off would be only too glad to fill it. True enough – but there is a *way* of doing it, a style of treatment Swiss through and through.

That's what Switzerland, to my mind, is all about. Style.

5
DARKEST CONTINENT
Morocco, Tunisia and The Gambia

It was one of those occasions, far from home, when I was wondering whether I was nuts to go on being a travel writer. Was it worth it, I asked myself, staring at the bedroom ceiling. Here I was, in a near-empty hotel out of season, the Mediterranean choppy at the end of the beach overlooked by my balcony, paying the penalty for eating a Moroccan dish which even my experienced stomach could not tackle.

I could imagine the unsympathetic grins of my office colleagues and their comments. 'The biter bit, eh? Always recommending people to try this, that and the other. "Eat the local food," you say. "You can get chop and chips at home – if that's all you want why leave Britain?" And what about all those precautions you warn your correspondents to take? Don't seem to have heeded them yourself, do you?' No point in my arguing that it is just as easy to get tummy upsets in Brighton as in Al Hoceima.

At that moment I doubt whether I could have convinced myself on the last point. In short, that night in Al Hoceima, I felt lousy. A bit homesick, too. And if you find it hard to believe that someone doing my job for so long ever gets homesick let me assure you there have been many instances when I have felt so disorientated – without any particularly logical reason for it, either – that I have cut trips short and taken the first plane out. Any travel writer, if he is honest, will admit he's done the same occasionally. Not necessarily, I may add, because the place one is visiting is so awful, but simply that even those of us who earn our living recommending other people where to go to enjoy themselves are only human.

Sleep was impossible. I was hot, uncomfortable, and the well-tried remedies I had fished from my medical kit did not seem to be working. Damn it all, damn the job! I'd a good mind to resign.

But then the phone rang – and from the moment I picked up receiver, worry about my digestion vanished. I was greeted by a flood of Spanish, delivered in a hoarse male voice. I tried the caller in English, I even hoped that somehow we could both make ourselves understood in French. But the Spanish tirade went on. And although I could understand no more than one word in twenty, it was plain that the tone was threatening.

Eventually I got the drift. Was my name Don Alfredo de something? I tried to convey a reply to the effect that I wasn't Don Alfredo anything. But the hoarse voice went on. Finally, I slammed down the receiver and found myself in such a fury of frustration that I never gave another thought to my stomach ache.

Sleepless as ever, I used my final technique to conquer insomnia – nothing will induce me to take sleeping-pills – and drew myself a hot bath. It worked – and I was off in minutes.

But I would never have so much as closed my eyes had I realized what the driver of my hired car from Tangier was to tell me at breakfast next morning. 'You had a call, sir, from a gentleman who only spoke Spanish, yes?'

I stared at him. 'That's right – how did you know?'

'He came to my lodgings, sir, and got me out of bed,' the driver said. He was highly experienced and his English was near-perfect. 'He asked me,' the man went on, ' "Who was that foreigner you brought with you? What is his name, what is he doing here, what nationality is he, and what else can you tell me about him?" '

'What was he – a policeman?' I asked, puzzled. 'Perhaps he thinks I'm something to do with opium smuggling out of the Rif.'

The driver looked embarrassed. 'Not a policeman, sir, exactly.'

'What did you tell him?' I demanded.

'That your name was De Fries; you were a British journalist writing about Morocco.'

'And?'

'He told me to say that he was sorry to have disturbed you, but he was acting on behalf of a lady who phoned him from Casablanca to trace a certain foreigner at your hotel and he found you were the only foreigner there.'

For a reason I cannot explain, I felt the hair prickle at the back of my neck. 'Who was this man?'

The driver looked more embarrassed than ever. 'Come on – out with it,' I said.

'The town assassin, sir.'

'THE WHAT?'

'The town assassin.'

'I think,' I said slowly, 'you'd better tell me all.' I had sat down to breakfast with little enough appetite; now I couldn't even face the rest of my coffee.

'He told me, sir,' the driver said, 'that this lady in Casablanca phoned him and let him know that her husband was a Spanish gentleman – '

'Don Alfredo?'

'Yes, sir. Something like that. She said: "He has been unfaithful to me and I want you to kill him." '

The sense of complete unreality which swept over me was heightened by the casual tone of the man. I began to wonder if I was dreaming.

'Do you know,' I said, struggling to stay calm, 'what you are saying? Do you know the difference between "kill" and "call"?' But I knew, even as I said it, that he did.

'Oh yes, sir,' the driver said earnestly. 'To call is what he did to you on the phone. To kill is . . . ' and he drew his forefinger across his throat.

I heard myself ask: 'But he was going to do more than call me if he decided I was Don Alfredo?'

'Yes, sir. He is a professional. The town assassin, as I said.'

'So, when he couldn't be sure from my talk with him, he traced you and you could confirm I wasn't Don Alfredo. Is that it?'

'Right, sir.'

'And what if,' I said, feeling distinctly faint now, 'you weren't around? What if I had come with a self-drive car?'

'It could have been very difficult, sir. He would have come to the hotel and killed you, sir.'

'Just like that?'

'Yes, sir.'

'And just as a matter of interest, what would have happened to him if the police had caught him afterwards?'

'Nothing, sir,' the driver said with a shrug. 'It was an affair of passion; lady hired him to do it.'

I stared past him out of the window. The sea was calm now, the sun was bright. It was going to be a warm Moroccan day, but I felt chilled. There was a long silence, broken only by the faint buzzing of insects. Then, with an effort, I forced myself out of my chair and walked deliberately to the reception desk and told them to make out my bill. 'We're going back to Tangier,' I said to the driver. He nodded glumly.

'And the programme, sir?'

'To hell with the programme.'

We didn't talk on that journey, which seemed to take an eternity.

I kept looking through the rear window to see if we were being followed, but the road behind us stretched back emptily through the haze.

I ordered the driver to take me to the office of the tour company where I had hired the car. The manager and his assistant were surprised to see me back early.

'Just answer the question,' I said. 'Is there a character in Al Hoceima who is regarded as the town assassin?'

Their jaws dropped, they looked at each other and then at me.

'Well?' I demanded.

'Er – er,' said the manager, gulping. 'How – how do you know about such matters, sir?'

'That's enough confirmation for me,' I said grimly. And told them the whole appalling story. During the telling they looked in every direction but mine.

'I am now,' I told them, 'going home. If you think for one

minute that I'm going to write about a town with a professional assassin ready to cut the throats of anyone for money and suggest it a good place to send British holidaymakers, you must be crazy.'

'You won't mention this bad matter in your newspaper, sir, will you?' pleaded the manager. 'It would be very bad for Moroccan tourism.'

'You can say that again,' I told him. 'But don't worry. I can't write about if for the simple reason that my office would think I'd been drinking and our readers simply wouldn't believe that such a thing could happen on a holiday coast in the twentieth century. Fortunately, I only went to Al Hoceima as a round-off for the rest of my piece. I've masses of stuff about areas a safe distance away, so Morocco will still get publicity from my trip out here. But, by God, it will want a bit of writing, in my present mood.'

A few hours later, while I was restlessly pacing the transit lounge at Madrid where I awaited a London plane, an acquaintance touched me on the shoulder. I jumped about a foot.

'Steady on, old man,' he said. 'Something wrong with the old nerves, then?'

All this happened a number of years ago. I've been back to Al Hoceima on a few occasions, found it a bigger, better organized place, crowded with tourists, and many people who have enjoyed holidays there would gape at me in disbelief if I told them this story.

Nor would I dream, by including it in this African chapter of a mainly light-hearted book, of trying to put anyone off a pleasant little holiday spot. But for an example of what can happen to someone like myself, travelling alone and out of season – plus an instance of the less jolly side of travel writing – this book isn't complete without it.

I've had marvellous times in Morocco. On the whole I enjoy the food and I'm a sucker for its exotic atmosphere. It is geographically speaking our nearest, most accessible bit of Eastern magic. Probably few travel writers have given so much space to it over the years and I look forward to many more visits there.

But Morocco isn't Europe – although Europe is visible from its shores. In virtually every respect that is surely the secret of its appeal. It's different – but I don't ever want it to be quite so different as I found it to be on that awful occasion in Al Hoceima.

I often wonder what happened to the faithless Don Alfredo.

There are wiseacres who will tell you knowingly that 'the Arabs' – a generalization that irritates me just as much as 'the Jews' – have a complicated system of society and a way of life few Westerners really understand. 'It's all baksheesh and bargaining, old man, take it from me. Everyone bribes everyone else. All very corrupt, they are.'

Now I don't regard it as part of my job to look deeply into the ways of societies I write about. For one thing I don't have the time or the space. For another, tourism is essentially superficial. If you want to know more about a country than tour operators and characters like me can possibly tell you, there are books, expert guides and lecturers galore.

But the passion for bargaining alleged to be rampant everywhere in the Arab world was impressed upon me before I took my first steps on North African soil. 'Do not,' I was told, 'ever accept the price they demand. Offer a lot less, they'll come down a bit and somehow you'll meet them and you'll save yourself money. They expect it, you see.'

Every tourist, I am sure, bargains when he goes to North Africa, to Greece, Turkey and points east. My wife does it to perfection. I must tell you now that not only do I get occasional stomach upsets abroad like most other people, but I can't bargain to save my life. A feeling of tiredness comes over me if a discussion about the price of any article I fancy goes on for more than a few seconds. Not only do I find the process of haggling very boring, but embarrassing, too.

So either I finish up paying a price which the know-alls will tell me later I was crazy to agree to – 'you were robbed, old chap; could have got it for half that amount myself' – or I leave without buying anything, however badly I may want it.

Making a show of walking out of a shop, I was told, could also force the shopkeeper to come to heel. So, on my first trip to Morocco, having failed to get the man to budge a single dirham, I muttered 'Ridiculous' and marched into the street.

He didn't bother to come out from behind his counter, he didn't call after me. And although I walked with painful slowness, with occasional glances back over my shoulder and my ears straining for a single pleading squeak of *'Effendi!'* or whatever, nothing happened. Well, almost nothing – so busy was I, not keeping my eyes to the front, that I was nearly flattened by a passing donkey cart. After that, I simply walked out of shops and never looked back, expecting nothing. And getting nothing if I departed from the price asked. That's how I operate now. All around me, in the meantime, are those happily convinced that they have forced the wretch selling the goods to do so on their own terms. Frankly, I must consider myself a disgrace to the Semitic tradition.

Which brings me to another alleged aspect of 'Arab' society – bribes. I may be ignorant of and ineffectual in bargaining, but I know all about bribes. Over the years attempts have been made to bribe me with money, booze, free travel, free accommodation, free sex. Even complete holidays ('bring your wife [nudge nudge] or a little lady, eh?'). I imagine all my fellow-travel writers could come up with similar tales.

But I'll bet no one but me has ever been offered the bribe of a hedgehog. The would-be bribers were two Moroccans scared that I would give an adverse report about them to their Ministry of Tourism. As it happened, their hedgehog offer stopped me doing just that. Not that I accepted the little prickly beast, mind you.

It all began some years ago when I arrived in Marrakech on the first stage of a romantic journey I had planned for myself to the Sahara fringes. I was to drive deep into the hinterland and eventually swing west to the Atlantic shore below Agadir and begin my return journey up the coast to Casablanca.

What I hadn't bargained for was the reluctance of the guide and driver I had arranged to follow such a route. By some administrative muddle in advance of my arrival, they had prepared themselves, presumably with much salivating, for a distinguished magazine writer specializing in gastronomy who was to be given a luxury tour of the imperial cities: Marrakech, Fez, Meknes, Rabat and so on.

Hair-shirted De Fries was another matter. They could not escape taking me out of Marrakech, but they were determined to sabotage the whole plan and exasperate me to such an extent that I would eventually order them in despair to return to base. There, with luck, the gourmandizing character they had been led to expect would be waiting and more than willing to overload them with largesse and the plentiful crumbs from his various dining-tables.

They put the first stage of their plan for destruction of my mission into operation a mere hour from the city. The driver braked to a halt, gave a loud groan, clutched his face and sank with sobs and sighs against his seat-back. It was a masterly performance.

The guide, with a suitably worried expression, turned to me. 'Sorry, sir,' he said. 'My friend has bad tooth. He will not be able to drive on.'

'I can offer him an aspirin,' I said.

'No, no, sir. I think it worse than that.'

I peered around. There was a tin-roofed shack, a solitary palm tree, a moth-eaten camel looking fed up with life, some fly-blown characters dozing in the dust – and precious little else.

'We can go back to Marrakech, sir,' said the guide eagerly. It was his very eagerness which made me suspicious.

'No we can't,' I said. 'This is ridiculous. If he can't drive why don't you take over?'

He was prepared for that. 'Impossible, sir,' he said, shaking his head mournfully. 'I'm guide. This is Government car. Only Government drivers can drive it.'

'But this is an emergency,' I said.

'Against regulation, sir.'

'Then I'll drive the damned thing,' I said.

'Not allowed, sir. You are foreigner.'

'Well, we're not going back,' I told him. 'You simply get your friend to stifle his pain until we reach the nearest town and let him see a dentist there.'

'No money, sir.'

'Then I'll pay.'

'We go back to Marrakech, sir.'

'No we don't. Tell him to drive on.'

'He won't, sir.'

'Well, I'm not stopping here.'

'Small hotel a few kilometres down road, sir.'

'Drive there and I'll have a look at it.'

For a man who allegedly spoke no English and was in acute pain, it was amazing how that driver responded. He started the car without a word and we drove to a crummy hotel in the middle of a crummy town no European in his senses would stay in for a moment.

'You've one hour,' I said grimly, 'to take him to a dentist.'

'No dentist here, sir.'

'Drive on then.'

'He can't, sir.'

'I'll take full responsibility for you breaking the regulations,' I said, determined now not to give an inch. 'You'll drive the car, he'll get in the back with me, we'll give him an aspirin and see what happens when we reach a town with a dentist.'

'Impossible, sir.'

'Then I'll hire a self-drive car.'

'No self-drive cars here, sir.'

'If you don't do as I say,' I said, 'I'll hire a bloody camel and ride that.'

Thank God he didn't call my bluff. But this last threat did seem to make an impression. The driver took the wheel again and we drove sullenly from one dusty town to another allegedly looking for dentists. It was incredible how many stories the guide told me of the difficulties he encountered in his search for this simple facility, returning from frequent absences during which the halted car was surrounded by characters who seemed to be wanting to sell me something. But as I said, I'm not a haggler.

The various versions of these difficulties as related by the guide included: the complete absence of dentists and too-busy-to-see-anyone dentists. Once even – and the sheer inventiveness took my breath away – 'Dentist here has toothache himself, sir. He can't see no one.'

Somehow, with each morning filled with the uncertainty that the safari could or would continue, I managed to fulfil my programme, and with a huge sense of relief, eventually found myself among the bright lights of Agadir.

'I shall be here for two days,' I told the guide. 'It's a big place, obviously crammed with dentists. You'll take your friend to one or another, you'll get his tooth fixed – I'll happily pay if you like – and when I'm ready to leave we leave and I don't want to hear another word about his bloody toothache. OK?'

'OK, sir.'

Two days later, we three jolly companions of the road met again. The driver was clutching his face in the time-honoured way and his groans were piteous to hear.

'I know, don't tell me,' I said. 'The dentist couldn't find his tools.'

'No, sir.'

'Well, then he's away treating that other dentist with toothache.'

'No, sir. Dentist gave my friend injection to take out tooth. But friend could not point out bad one, so took three out. Now he has sore mouth and can't drive.'

'Right,' I said briskly. 'I'll simply hire myself a car, drive up the road to Casablanca and give one hell of a report about the pair of you to your bosses. Heaven knows what they'll do to you. Pity I shan't be around to see it. They'll probably take all his teeth out and yours, too, I shouldn't wonder.'

Silence. Then: 'Please get in car, sir. We go to Casablanca.'

Not a word was exchanged as we headed north; not a groan from up front; not a sudden braking, no histrionic sobs, nothing. Then, a few miles short of Casablanca Airport, in a desolate place without so much as a blade of grass to be seen, the driver stopped beside a small dusty boy selling hedgehogs at the roadside.

There was a conversation in Arabic between boy and driver. The guide turned to me, smiling. 'What's going on now?' I demanded.

'My friend make you a present, sir. To take home. Lovely hedgehog, sir.'

82

The boy came to the passenger window and thrust the creature under my nose. I withdrew out of reach hastily – and thinking hard. A scheme of sweet revenge entered my head – far more effective and satisfying to myself than any angry report to the Ministry of Tourism.

'Tell your friend,' I said slowly, 'that I am very grateful for his offer, but I would have some difficulty getting the hedgehog into England. We have strict regulations, you see. Also, we have many hedgehogs in Britain already. Cars squash them all over the roads. But perhaps your friend would like a hedgehog as a pet for his children. Or for dinner maybe. So I'll tell you what I'll do. I'll buy a hedgehog for your friend.'

Beams all round.

'There's just a condition or two, however,' I went on, poker-faced. 'It's the matter of carrying the hedgehog. I'll buy it if you can provide a suitably large tin with air holes in the lid, a saucer of milk and some lettuce.'

Beams faded. 'Where – where we could get such things here, sir?' the guide said, bewildered. 'There's nothing for miles.'

'That's your problem,' I said.

'But, sir, hedgehog no need milk, no need lettuce. It can travel in car.'

'Like hell it can – it'll spread fleas everywhere,' I said.

'In boot then.'

'I don't want my luggage flea-bitten, thank you.'

'Oh, sir.'

'Oh sir nothing. If you can't meet my terms, tell your friend to drive on.'

I threw the boy a dirham – the price of the hedgehog I wasn't allowing in the car. We drove on to the airport. And I left them dismayed and anxious as to what would happen next. What would I tell their ministry? The answer was: nothing. They'd given me a lot of annoyance, they had realized they'd overdone it, they had offered me the most peculiar bribe ever, but had no taker. I had paid them back for the nuisance in my own way. And if I left them wriggling with uncertainty for a few days, all to the good.

Perhaps I was being cruel. But at least I had given that poor hedgehog a break. Like me, he didn't deserve that driver.

Moroccan acquaintances have been appalled at my story of the threatening phonecall from the sinister character in Al Hoceima and have roared with laughter about the hedgehog affair. Neither, they have been at great pains to assure me, could possibly be called typical of what the visitor to Morocco – and there has been tourism there on a large scale for decades – could encounter from Ramadan to Ramadan. I'm happy enough to believe them. As I said earlier, there's a lot to relish in Morocco. I still get a kick out of spending an evening in one of those traditional restaurants which grace the imperial cities – taking my seat on a divan before a low table beneath a lofty ceiling supported by graceful columns gleaming with multi-coloured stones; having rose water poured over my hands by a pretty girl dressed like Scheherazade's handmaiden; being served the best of native cuisine while sensuous dancers whirl around me in flickering lamplight to pipes and drums, and contortionists and jugglers do impossible feats.

One dish I always ask for in such an exotic setting is unlikely to be included on any half-board arrangement you can buy as part of a package tour – although one or two of the more up-market operators might have succeeded in breaking through the price barrier to make the serving of it possible. Pastilla is *the* classic, *the* most elegant Moroccan speciality: multiple layers of paper-thin pastry wrapped around baby pigeon and hardboiled eggs, flavoured with cinnamon. To Westerners it is an acquired taste. I acquired that taste many years ago and no visit to Morocco is complete for me without my having pastilla at least once.

But pastilla just doesn't work if a restaurant prepares it with chicken and not pigeon. So imagine my disappointment when in one of my favourite Moroccan speciality eating-places – at a leading hotel in an imperial city – the waiter informed me that there was only the chicken version available.

Next day, I tackled the hotel manager, a solemn, highly professional Swiss. He spread his hands in despair. 'No pigeons, *Herr* De Fries,' he said, 'A shortage of them, I fear. But let me at least show you around der hotel. We haff several new vings since you were last here.'

The new sections of the hotel were tasteful, copying faithfully the Arabian Nights design of the whole marvellously luxurious place. You reached the spendid new apartments through a series of tiny courtyards.

The manager led the way – and the pigeons, dozens of them, gave him hell each time we emerged into the open. They spattered his expensive light-weight suit with the accuracy of Stukas on the warpath. They forced him into a crouching position and as desperately he tried to clean himself up with a handkerchief to keep at least a semblance of his former smartness, he went on expressing regret about the pastilla . . .

'Der trouble ist, ve don't haff enough pigeons.'

Oddly, the pigeons entirely ignored me. But then I wasn't in the habit of baking their offspring in a pie.

Tunisia has its food specialities too. The ubiquitous brik, for example: a soft cooked egg in thin pastry designed to squirt yolk in your eye or down your shirt front unless bitten or cut into with care. But the country's tourist ministry, anxious to show visitors that old French connections have not been entirely forgotten when it comes to *cuisine*, persuaded me one night to sample international-style cooking at the national hotel school's restaurant.

The card, proferred by an anxious-to-please young waiter, was impressive. 'You really do all these things?' I asked the waiter.

He beamed. 'Yes, sir,' he said proudly. 'All of them.'

'Splendid,' I said, 'we'll start with the lobster.'

'No lobster, sir.'

'The crab then.'

'No crab, sir.'

'The sole.'

'No sole, sir.'

'The sweetbreads,' I said, deciding it must be a bad day for fish.

'No sweetbreads, sir.'

There was also no paté de foie gras, no kidneys, no oeufs en cocotte, no vol-au-vent, gazpacho, risotto, not even humble consommé or quiche lorraine. I'd come to the end of the list of starters.

'Well, what *have* you got?'

'Salad, sir.'

In trepidation I turned to the main items.

'Duck, I think,' I said.

'No duck, sir.'

'Coq au vin.'

'No coq au vin, sir.'

'Chicken breasts in cream.'

'No chicken breasts, sir.'

'Entrecôte, then.'

'No entrecôte, sir.'

The continuing list of items the pupils at that hotel school could not prepare for me that night made me ravenous. I won't list them all here – they would make your mouth water, too – but it would have been a fantastic meal if I could only have got my knife and fork into a tiny fraction of what was proudly displayed on that card.

Finally, I said: 'OK. Tell me what you *can* offer.'

'Lamb chops, sir.' I cast a gloomy look at the next table. Two minute charred-looking bones virtually devoid of meat were being regarded with a distinct lack of enthusiasm by the poor chap who had just ordered them with a rather tired salad.

'I think not,' I said. 'How about an omelette or a soufflé?'

'No omelettes or soufflés, sir.'

'Of course you have no omelettes or soufflés *at the moment*,' I said testily. 'But surely you must have eggs?'

'Yes, sir.'

'Then make me an omelette.'

'No omelettes tonight, sir.'

I gave up. 'Bring me the lamb bones then.'

'The lamb chops, sir?'

'All right, the lamb chops. Forget the salad and I don't much like the look of your greasy chips, either.'

Later he handed me a mile-long dessert list.

'Waste of time going through it, I'm sure,' I said, trying to quell my appetite with bread and rather rancid butter. 'So how about a Norwegian omelette?'

'No Norwegian omelettes, sir.'

'The ship hasn't arrived from Norway, I suppose?' I said.

'I believe that is the case, sir. We can do nothing until the ship comes.'

'No cheese, of course.'

'No cheese, sir.'

'What do you suggest then?'

'Fruit, sir.'

'What fruit?'

'There's one portion of water-melon left, sir.'

I settled for coffee. Later I went back to my hotel and was squirted with a brik.

'No man needs two pens,' boomed my river-boat captain.

'This man does,' I said.

I began to wonder just how many more times I would have to tell him that I wasn't going to give up one of the two pens he could see clipped to my shirt pocket. Heaven knows there had been enough time for him to make repeated hints and downright demands for one of them. We had been stuck, for what seemed an eternity, on a sweltering West African morning, moored beside the ancient crumbling waterfront of Banjul, capital of The Gambia, while an argument raged as to which two passengers were to get off to prevent overloading.

Nearby was the only other craft then available for trips up the Gambia river – a sleek, streamlined air-conditioned yacht belonging to the tiny country's president. It seemed that when His Excellency wasn't using it, the Gambian version of the *Britannia* was available for tourists – but only when the demand for the tourist department's solitary vessel exceeded the latter's capacity by a certain number.

Had about eight more tourists booked for the trip that morning, there would have been no problem. But we were only overloaded by *two* and that, it seemed, was not sufficient reason to justify our transfer to the presidential yacht. So those two had to get off before we could start. But which two?

I must say I would have given the earth to make the passage in that cool-looking yacht. There was virtually no cover on the launch decks and the heat was getting worse every minute.

Tempers were frayed. Most of my fellow-passengers were black Americans, and for them a trip up river to the village featured in the best-seller *Roots* was a virtual pilgrimage none of them wanted to miss.

From that village, the author of *Roots* claimed, his ancestor had been kidnapped by slavers and carried across the Atlantic. Understandably quick to realize the tourist potential of the little place, the Gambian authorities had turned the village into their country's major attraction away from fabulous beaches and newly built hotels. The more camera-loaded tourists who could be persuaded up river, to thrust tips into the eager hands of village children and pay dearly for each turn of the corn grinding pole by women who had virtually become full-time tourist department employees, the better.

But today, before the exercise could begin, two would-be passengers had to volunteer to walk the shaky plank back to the Banjul jetty and my captain had all the time in the world to drive me crazy with his rumbles of: 'No man needs two pens.'

As the morning wore on, I felt so desperately hot and anxious to get away from him and his entreaties that I was on the point of volunteering to cut down the boat's overload by half. I realized, however, that the same chaos, the same nagging, could occur next day and the next. And I certainly couldn't tackle a feature on The Gambia without spending at least a few hours on the river.

Meanwhile, the arguments between tour organizers and passengers continued apace. 'Are yuh kidding, man? I get off? I come all this godammed way to see this godammed village my family came from as slaves – oh yes they did, man, don't dammwell argue with me, man – and you want to push me off the godammed boat. Ask someone else. Don't you move an inch there, Martha. We're staying. Let some other folk get off.'

At long last, to everyone's relief, a couple were finally harried/shamed into volunteering to go ashore for the sake of the floating community, who were thus saved from being precipitated among the crocodiles. They looked Scandinavian – thus emotionally uninvolved – and suitably saintly and smug at the sacrifice they had made. The rest of us gave them a feeble cheer.

We chugged away, and no sooner had the captain satisfied himself that we were in no danger of dragging the rotting remains of Banjul jetty in our wake than he was at me again for one of those wretched pens.

He kept up his campaign at regular intervals for the whole morning. He was still after a gift of a pen when we finally came in sight of Banjul again. He didn't get it of course – I don't give away the tools of my trade when I can't guarantee to find a replacement, and even cheap pens like mine were obviously rarities in The Gambia. But I couldn't help admiring his persistence.

'You can only write with one pen at a time,' he said.

'I have two pens,' I said wearily, 'because if one runs out, I have another to use.'

'But that means' – with a huge grin – 'that you are then just a one-pen man.'

'I know,' I said. 'And no man needs two pens.'

'Right. So give me a pen.'

'Goodbye, captain.'

I didn't tell him that I thought they were making such a mess of going alongside that it was plain his boat needed two captains. He was bigger than I was.

The Gambia is a desperately poor little country. Tourism is vital – the remainder of the economy consists largely and literally of peanuts. Back in the heady days of the post-war Attlee government, The Gambia was seen in Whitehall as an essential part of the grandiose Groundnut Scheme. Before that collapsed in ignominy and ridicule, millions were poured in from the coffers filled by British tax-payers, and safari-suited civil servants swarmed all over the country. They and the former colonial community left behind a tradition for such apt fare in sky-high temperatures as British nursery-style bread and butter pudding, jam roly-poly and fish and chips. Today, British package tourists blacken in the sun, stuff themselves full of cabinet pudding – and marvel. Those old enough to remember find themselves filled with nostalgia for Empire and take the mosquitoes as a matter of course.

Naturally, bargaining is 'rampant'. Beware the natives who want to sell you model elephants. One, impeccably dressed in the sort of old-cut European dark suit that goes with bread and butter puddings, asked if he could take the armchair opposite mine in the lounge of my hotel. I'd just been congratulating myself on still having two pens and was rounding off my trip on the river with a typically Gambian afternoon repast of tea and Dundee cake.

'Is that tea pot empty, man?'

'Probably not,' I say. 'But I've finished with it.'

'Do you mind if I have some?'

'Help yourself . . . but you'll need a clean cup.'

'No matter, I'll use yours.'

Fills cup and drinks tea with noisy smacking of lips. Then:

'Would you like to buy an elephant, man.'

'Not today, thanks.'

'I have him right here.' Produces with chuckle large package, unwraps to show beautifully carved elephant but whole effect ruined by ghastly ashtray protruding from model's back.

'What about £60 for him, man?' (I'll translate into sterling to protect the innocent.)

'Not interested, thanks.'

'Fifty.'

'Forget it.'

'Forty.'

'Sorry.'

'How much will you give me, man? Is a wonderful elephant, this.'

'Not interested.'

'I'm not coming any lower, man.'

'I'm not asking you to, am I?'

'What about twenty, man?'

'What about me giving you a pound to go away?'

'I accept. May I just see if there's any more tea in the pot first? And could you spare one of your pens? No? Oh.'

In seconds, his place is taken by a poker-faced Far Eastern gentleman in immaculate blue blazer and knife-edged-creased flannels. Bows politely to me before sitting. He has a miniature photograph of himself on his lapel with hieroglyphics written underneath.

'I from Korea. Where you from?'

'Britain.'

'Ah, so. Tourist?'

'Journalist.'

'Me journalist too. Come with group.' Waves in direction of large number of other Eastern gentlemen dressed in exactly the same way, each bearing a photograph on their lapels and all looking remarkably similar. 'My colleagues – all journalists. What you write about?'

'Tourism,' I tell him.

'Ah, so. Tourism – not important subject. We write about how liberated Africa casting off imperialistic yoke.'

'Let me guess,' I say, stung by his scorn for tourism. 'What part of Korea do you come from? Would it, could it, be the North?'

Smiles, gives neat mini-bow from sitting position. 'The People's Socialist Republic of North Korea.'

'Tell me,' I say, 'just how many pens do they let you take out of your country?'

Puzzlement. 'Pens? Oh, two. Must carry one spare.'

'No man needs two pens,' I tell him.

6
THE FAR END OF THE MED
Greece, Turkey and Israel

I'm always intrigued by the completely different attitudes adopted towards travel writers by the tourist authorities of countries at each extreme end of the political spectrum.

On the Far Left – I've the Soviets principally in mind, but some of their Slav minions faithfully copy them – we are regarded with the utmost surliness and suspicion. I have the feeling that so convinced are they that Britain will, quite inevitably, fall into the revolutionary net one day that it doesn't really matter what impression their treatment makes on me – although of course they do recognize travel journalists as useful in persuading compatriots to spend much-needed hard currency.

But when you visit a tourist country which has slipped to the Far Right, the attentions of the authorities, desperate to get a sympathetic picture of themselves to the outside world, can be positively embarrassing. There is nothing, but nothing, that the powers will not do to make you feel that everyone has sadly misjudged them and they are really a bunch of decent folk ready to beam a welcome to tourists at all times. The red carpet laid out for you is often so plush that there is a real danger of your travel-stained suitcase vanishing into it.

Greece under the Colonels was just like that. I was probably the first travel writer from a major source of Greece's foreign tourism to go there after the junta had taken over. The tourist trade had been devastated overnight. Scandinavians who habitually crammed Rhodes and other major centres had cancelled bookings in their thousands. British tourists were dithering, British press comments on the new regime from the mildly reproving to the vitriolic. Red mullet were virtually begging to be caught by Aegean fishermen on the grounds that the sea was becoming overcrowded through not enough concentrated fishing – as there didn't seem enough people about to eat the catches. Aubergines, earmarked for use by the moussaka industry, were rotting away in heaps.

I was summoned to the Foreign Ministry in Athens to find myself confronted by a panel of grim-looking characters seated around a long table. 'Mr De Fries,' their spokesman said. 'What are you going to tell your readers about our country?'

'I shall write what I see,' I said.

'And that is?'

'The sun is shining, the sea is blue. From the purely touristic point of view Greece is still Greece. After all, people who are concerned about your politics will stay away, whatever writers like me say. But those who simply want a holiday here will come. And frankly I don't see why they shouldn't.'

'You have seen no political interference with the tourist trade?' they wanted to know.

'None,' I said truthfully. 'And if I did and I thought it to the detriment of British tourists, I would tell my editor that we couldn't possibly go on advocating Greek holidays.'

'Have you seen any soldiers in the streets, Mr De Fries?'

'No more than usual.'

'Heard any machine-gun fire, seen any tanks?'

'One burst of machine-gun fire,' I said, 'and I would get the first plane out. You can't mix tourism and civil war. I'm not a war correspondent after all.'

'Will you please tell your readers that there are no tanks in the streets and no gunfire?'

'I don't think,' I said, 'you can direct me what to write. There certainly must have been gunfire recently. Let us just hope I don't hear any myself. I would hate to have made a wasted journey here.'

Nods of understanding around the table.

I rose. 'Can I go now?' I asked.

'One question, Mr De Fries,' the spokesman said. He leaned

forward confidentially. 'Have you any complaints about our tourist facilities? We would like to improve anything you think is not quite right.'

'I think maybe that your guided excursions are too expensive,' I said.

He picked up a pencil. 'Which ones?' His attitude became strictly military, curt. Suddenly I had an awful vision of my being responsible for untold numbers of excursion-firm executives being led out to the firing-squads.

'Please don't ask me to be specific,' I said hastily. 'It's just a general observation.' Thankfully, I made my escape.

But for each of my subsequent visits to Greece under the military regime there was no escaping the fact that travel writers were regarded as VIPs, even if sometimes arrangements went haywire. I was normally conducted around by a bossy little woman who, whenever I wanted to know something technical or historic, would reply with irritation that she was not a guide and I should look it up in a book. She also infuriated my wife by tickling her under the chin and then making such a mess of organizing a sweaty climb to the Parthenon that she contrived to get Jennifer to that magnificent place just as it was about to close for the evening.

Her boss of bosses – the Colonel of Greek Tourism himself – was not content, however, to leave everything in the hands of his representative without question. I was astonished to discover that whenever I booked into a hotel to start a visit to another region of Greece, however distant from Athens, he had already been on the phone warning them to make sure I had a comfortable room. He would then follow this up with a personal call to me. 'Is everything all right?' he would demand.

'Yes, thank you, Colonel,' I would say. 'The room is very pleasant.'

'Are the tourist office people co-operating with you in every way?'

'In every way, thank you, Colonel.'

The hotel staff were so twitchy, that I was almost afraid to find fault with anything in case one adverse comment drove them to nervous breakdowns. The local tourist offices looked on me with positive awe. Only one official was bold enough, I remember, to make the feeblest joke about a situation I found embarrassing. 'Your daddy's been on the phone about you today, and he was on the phone yesterday too,' he told me. 'I think he must love you very much, your daddy.'

'Well,' I replied, 'whatever Daddy said, just you make sure I get a room bill in the normal way.' I had to keep fighting to pay – hotels wanted to give me free accommodation.

I had constantly to assure everyone in the tourist business that, far from being a personal friend of the colonel's, I had never set eyes on him in my life. I also found it necessary to say that I was simply doing my job as a journalist, writing about tourism in a country which – colonels or no colonels – was justly famous for it. Whatever government was in power would make no difference to me.

Eventually I did meet my daddy. Once and only once. I was on the island of Kos. He was flying back to Athens on the plane which had brought Jennifer and myself for a stay, so the airport meeting was brief. 'I am very pleased to meet you at last,' he said, looming over me. 'Please come to Greece many times.'

'Thank you for your kind attention,' I said. I couldn't match his ramrod military stance and wondered whether I had been expected to salute if not click my heels.

He flew back to Athens and we found ourselves in the hotel suite he had just vacated. Treasonably, we thought it mediocre. 'But this is the colonel's suite,' the horrified manager said. 'And the hotel is new. He only opened it yesterday.'

We decided, for various reasons, that we hated the place, checked out as soon as possible and found ourselves another hotel. I wondered if I had thus queered my pitch with the colonel. But at least I had shown my independence.

I doubt whether anyone would have dared tell Daddy that I didn't think his hotel suite good enough. Anyway, he certainly showed no signs of being offended. His solicitous calls continued. And with due ceremony I was eventually presented on his behalf with a replica of a drinking-cup found in a Macedonian tomb. A letter accompanied it, beginning: 'In recognition of your services to Greek tourism, it gives me great pleasure . . . '

Three months later I received an identical letter. Lo and

behold Daddy had decided to present me with a replica of a drinking-cup found in a Macedonian tomb. It looked exactly like the first one – except that it was mounted and complete with a plaque which described me as being a good friend of Greece.

'If that just doesn't show how much he values friendship,' my wife commented. 'He's obviously forgotten the first cup he sent.'

That first cup we donated as a prize to be competed for in a horse show. The second I still possess, the plinth being found suitable to stick on and thus preserve a press cutting relating to Daddy's final fall from grace when his fellow-colonels found he had been dabbling in illegal meat imports from what was then Rhodesia. Thus he was safely tucked up in prison – already there and, as it were, keeping the cells warm for his mates – when democracy finally brought the military regime to a timely end.

But so long as Daddy was in charge, I have to admit that his very name worked wonders in emergencies. That bossy little woman minion of his was a sort of personal standard-bearer on his behalf the length and breadth of the country. With her throwing her arms about and shrieking threats and imprecations if this, that or the other wasn't done immediately, no obstacle was too great to be overcome. If a storm blew up and an inter-island ferry was cancelled and thus interfered with my programme, the service was promptly restored with a green-faced De Fries and said bossy escort the only passengers. If a remote country taverna was short of a particular dish on the day I was there, somehow that dish was produced. If a temple closed temporarily while the guardian went off for a snooze under an olive tree in the heat of the afternoon, that sleep was interrupted and the gates unlocked for me – only the Parthenon itself defied her efforts.

Once she even called out a sizeable portion of the Greek army to our rescue. The Peloponnese weather had turned nasty. The wind howled, the rain lashed our windscreen. Our driver, plainly an anti-junta man, loathed her, loathed me and the world. When we bounced into a flooded pothole and a great puddle reared over us and stopped the motor he made no attempt to put things to rights. He just sat there, hunched moodily over the wheel, deaf to her threats.

For thirty minutes she harangued him without result. It looked as if it was going to turn out to be her only failure to date. In the meantime the sky was getting blacker, the rain and wind harder. 'We're never going to get back to Athens tonight at this rate,' I told her. 'He seems to have given up altogether. Perhaps we can thumb a lift?'

I knew that was a remote possibility to say the least. For the whole time we had been stuck in that pothole, there hadn't been a single vehicle passing us. All we had seen were sheep, endless sheep. As each one moved slowly past the car it stared in and uttered: 'Ba-a-a.' Nor was there a solitary house in sight at which to summon help – just cypress groves and mountains dimly outlined in the growing murk of the afternoon.

Now although I had no more desire than she did to continue sitting in that wind-buffeted vehicle in the middle of nowhere and would in any other circumstances have insisted on our getting out and at least making a move on foot in the direction in which we were pointed – even if it meant getting soaked and walking perhaps for miles – I decided ungallantly to be as unhelpful as the driver was and just see what bossy-boots would do.

What in fact she did in the end, it must be admitted, was impressive in its results, however unpromising it appeared at the onset. She wrapped her flimsy raincoat around her, seized her equally flimsy umbrella – which looked more like a parasol for a pampered poodle than a device able to afford any sort of protection in the middle of a Peloponnese monsoon – and alighted in the middle of the sheep. She cleared a passage through them waving her umbrella, but when she tried to open the little thing in the teeth of the gale, it predictably blew inside out and she threw it away in a fury. In seconds the sheep had closed in again and I soon lost her from sight through the streaming windows.

I was left with the morose driver who couldn't speak a word of English. So there was enforced silence, broken only by the drumming of rain on the roof and the ba-a-as from those interminable sheep.

98

The afternoon wore drearily on towards evening. By my watch she was away just over an hour. Then she returned, soaked but triumphant, riding in a staff car with tabbed, immaculate officers. I couldn't identify their ranks, but it seemed that the most junior was a major. Behind came two mammoth trucks filled with soldiers of an engineering regiment.

The officers saluted me smartly, the soldiers clustered around the bonnet. Tools were produced, the engine started, the car was eased out of the pothole. More salutes, smiles all round, and off we headed towards Athens.

'What did you do – stop them on the road?' I asked her.

She swelled with pride and self-importance. 'No – I found a farm lorry, ordered the driver to take me to the nearest barracks,' said the Colonel of Tourism's personal representative. 'I demanded to see the officer in charge. I told him who I was, who I was accompanying.'

'And you mentioned the colonel's name of course.'

'Of course, and the officer in charge at once broke off his conference, ordered his adjutant to take out a party to us.'

'What was his own rank – general of course?'

'Yes – a full general.'

Now somehow I don't think a Greek army general would respond today in quite that way to a tourist who breaks down on a lonely country road. General mobilization in miniature for such a reason is probably no more the Greek army style than it is the style among peacetime armies anywhere. But while I have to admit that in a dictatorship it is very useful indeed when it comes to exerting pressure to be able to namedrop – not to say intimidate – and we were at least assured of reaching our destination that same day, I think I prefer Greece as you'll find her now – her old, rather haphazard but well-intentioned self. I'm quite sure too that if you did have the misfortune to break down and could reach a hamlet, everyone there would be only too happy to try to help. Even if they took a good deal longer about it.

If it is any consolation to those who smart at the memory of at least one disastrous trip abroad as a result of mistreatment at the hands of the travel industry, let me assure you that you are in good company. I was once the victim of a none too bright and poorly organized – plain incompetent would be too harsh a description – tour operator combined with an unscrupulous hotel management. When it came to the inevitable blow-up, the latter admitted their perfidy with cool indifference. The managing director of the tour company, however, was completely unable to give me a coherent explanation of why everything had gone so horribly wrong. The very thought of the whole affair still makes me wince.

It all began some years ago when I read in a brochure of an amazingly cheap deal offered by a company specializing in Turkey. Some genius had dreamed up a title for a winter weekend in Istanbul redolent of the Arabian Nights, of Scheherazade, of Ali Baba and the Forty Thieves. Now you can't go much further from home for a weekend than Istanbul and when I read that the deal included scheduled flight, transfers to and from the airport, accommodation and breakfast in a hotel belonging to a leading American chain, a free drink and admission to the hotel's nightclub show and even a box of Turkish Delight, I thought I was on to something good to recommend to readers.

So I flew to Istanbul for my winter weekend. The only difference between the arrangements I put in hand for myself and those which would be made by the operator concerned for anyone who wanted to take the deal was that I did not buy the package as a whole because I was stopping off *en route* to do another story. So I paid the normal return air fare from London – which alone made the cost of the whole package sound like peanuts – and the full rate at the hotel in Istanbul featured in the operator's brochure.

What I had specifically asked the tour operator to ensure for me, however, was a room of the type used on the package deal and admission to the nightclub. And naturally I expected to find my box of Turkish Delight waiting.

There was admittedly something faintly comic about a hater of Turkish Delight telephoning from my room as soon as I was shown into it and complaining to the reception that there wasn't so much as one quivering piece of oversweetened jelly to be seen.

'Later. It comes later, sir. When you go to bed,' I was told.

A much more severe blow was struck when I asked what time the nightclub opened.

'We don't have nightclub, sir. Closed last August. We have only disco.'

'But this brochure,' I argued, 'says there's supposed to be a show.'

'Yes, we have show. We flash coloured lights on the disco walls.'

'There's something very wrong here,' I said. 'Where's the manager?'

'Not here, sir.'

'Then where's the tour operator's representative?'

'His office is closed until tomorrow, sir.'

I created enough uproar in the next hour for a senior hotel official to put in an appearance. He insisted on taking me to dinner; it was, he said smoothly, too, too bad that the tour operator's rep was not about. I told him my reason for not wishing to dine at the hotel's main restaurant. It would be pricey and international and I wanted to dine cheaply and in Turkish style.

'No cost to you,' said the hotel man.

'With respect, that's not the point. It has to be reasonably priced for Mr and Mrs Smith. I have to demonstrate that it is. It has also to be Turkish. Not much sense coming all this way for the weekend to be served steak and chips.'

'Ah, I understand,' said the Turkish gentleman, suave as ever. 'We have Turkish food. And prices are very cheap, you will see. We also have entertainment.'

'I'd rather dine out with entertainment,' I said.

'Please, Mr De Fries. Do not offend me. Eat in the hotel. Your readers will be tired after such a long journey. They would not want to go out on the first night.'

'Well, let's try your coffee shop then.'

'No, sir. I would not hear of it. Come along.'

Suddenly I was weary of arguing. I let him take me to the main restaurant. He was right – there *was* entertainment. An

101

elderly man playing listlessly on an elderly piano a programme of elderly tunes.

The menu – about a mile long and almost entirely international – did not even bear a price list. This all confirmed my worst suspicions.

Deliberately and much to the manager's chagrin, I ordered a basic Turkish meal: starters with salad, kebab as main course; baklava and a small carafe of wine. It was the sort of repast you would emphatically not order in such grand surroundings.

I then had a battle to wrench the price details of my choice from the manager. Finally and with great reluctance he did some calculations. I translated the amount of Turkish lire into sterling – £20. Roughly three times the amount you would pay for such a meal in more humble but quite acceptable establishments outside.

'I don't call that cheap,' I said. 'It's a sizeable chunk of the whole price the operator charges for the weekend here, flight and all.'

'It's cheap,' he insisted, waving an airy hand around the room. 'Lovely furnishings, view of the Bosphorus. The piano –'

'To say nothing of the flashing lights in the disco,' I said acidly.

'That's extra, of course,' was the reply.

I ignored the disco and went moodily to my room. The Turkish Delight had been delivered: two minute squares on my pillow, with a printed note attached wishing me goodnight in ten languages.

Next morning I confronted the tour operator's rep. I waved the brochure in his face. 'Everything here seems to be rubbish,' I said, 'except the name of the hotel.'

'Name of hotel wrong, sir,' he replied.

'WHAT?'

'We no longer use this hotel, sir. Not since August when the nightclub closed.'

Breathing hard, I asked what hotel the operator *did* use. The rep named one of a rival chain a short distance away.

'Why didn't someone tell me this?' I demanded.

'No idea, sir.'

'So what happens if people get this brochure and book up?

They think they are going to the hotel featured in it.'

'We make sure they get the right one.'

'So why didn't *I* get the right one?'

'You are not really a client of ours, sir.'

'But why haven't your people replaced this brochure?'

He shrugged. I pounced on the blandly smiling hotel man.

'If you knew this operator was no longer using your hotel why didn't you tell me so last night?' I demanded.

'We think we should have the business back,' he said. 'It was stolen from us. When we heard you were a journalist we thought that if you wrote about our hotel the operator would have to return the contract to us.'

'I give up,' I said in despair.

At that moment I wished *I* could write to a travel editor and complain. People are always doing it.

The Sea of Galilee – really a huge lake – is a lovely place. And the very sight of it can arouse emotions, whether you are Christian, Jew or Muslim. The weather was gorgeous and I had so far enjoyed every moment of my day. From the waterfront of Tiberius, backed by tall modern buildings, I had taken a morning ferry to the far shore to lunch at a kibbutz restaurant off the most famous dish in this corner of Israel – St Peter's fish. And to eat it by the waters of the Parable of the Loaves and Fishes is really something . . .

Later I wandered happily along the shore before boarding a ferry for the return trip. I lit my pipe and puffed away contentedly; the whole atmosphere of the place had got to me and I felt so happy to be there. It was one of those occasions when I wouldn't have swapped my job for any other.

The only gloomy aspect of it all, I thought, was that a couple of burly characters were riding shotgun, protecting a school outing from any fanatic tempted to take a potshot at them – just to remind the world that there had been a Six Day War when those waters, then so close to the Syrian frontier, were deadly indeed.

When I felt the blow on the back of my neck I thought the worst had happened. It was hard enough to send me pitching

103

out of my seat and on to my face. Confusion broke out behind me. There seemed some sort of struggle going on, curses and strange squawks filled what had been the peaceful air.

Someone was leaning over me and speaking in Hebrew. He switched to American-English. 'Are you OK, bud?'

'I don't know really,' I heard myself say. Cautiously I felt the back of my neck. No blood. Not even broken skin, just tenderness. I levered myself up on my elbows and stared at the bodyguard's face. His eyes were filling with tears. Of laughter. He couldn't restrain himself a second longer. He burst out into a great bellow of mirth.

'Thought you'd been shot, did yuh? Take a look at what hit yuh, friend,' he spluttered.

I turned. The passenger who had been sitting behind me was forcing a furious and very large turkey back into the sack on his lap from which it had struggled free. 'Gave you some *schloch* with his wing, that bird,' chortled the bodyguard. 'Mighty tough bird that, mighty tough.'

His laughter spread to everyone on the ferry. The children in particular were in hysterics. Only two people were still straight-faced: the owner of the turkey and myself.

'Do you speak English?' I demanded of him, even more angry now than the turkey. I admit freely that nothing puts me in a temper faster than fright.

He nodded, still panting from his exertions. 'All I can say,' I told him, 'is that I hope when that bloody bird is let out again he'll give you a black eye.'

But the laughter around me was too infectious to ignore, despite my neckache. I just had to join in. And seeing me laugh, the poor turkey owner started to grin, too.

There are few surer ways of making yourself unpopular as a visitor to Israel than even as to hint that the country might be unsafe for tourists, but I just couldn't resist saying as much at the Foreign Press Department of the Israeli Ministry of Tourism in Jerusalem next day.

'Dangerous country, this,' I said solemnly.

The formidable lady who greeted me there whipped the smile of welcome from her face in a trice. Her eyes narrowed. She waved me to a chair, her expression grim. 'What exactly do you mean?' she demanded.

'I was the victim of an attack,' I told her, still poker-faced. 'On the Sea of Galilee.'

She picked up a pencil and pulled a notepad before her. 'Precisely where?'

'On the back of my neck – it's still damned sore, too.'

'No, no,' she snapped impatiently. 'Where on the Sea of Galilee?'

'About half a mile out of Tiberius,' I said. She began writing rapidly.

'I was hit on my neck,' I went on, 'by a turkey. And I claim a world record. Who else has ever been attacked by a turkey on the Sea of Galilee, I should like to know?'

She didn't laugh at this revelation, as I had expected. She merely raised her eyebrows.

'What nationality was the turkey?' she asked. There wasn't a hint of humour in the way she put that question either. I burst out laughing. She wasn't amused. 'It's not funny, Mr De Fries. I need to know every detail.'

'You're not serious, surely?'

'Of course I am,' she insisted.

'Look,' I said, struggling to be serious again and beginning to wish I hadn't started the subject. 'How would I know the thing's nationality? It simply broke out of a sack and hit me with its wing.'

She put down her pencil and stared at me. 'With its wing?' she repeated.

'With its wing.'

Enlightenment dawned on her face. She grinned. 'You mean,' she said slowly, 'it was a turkey-*bird*? That's a different matter.'

'What did you think I meant?'

'I thought you were telling me a *tourist* hit you. That's our name in Israel for tourists. Turkeys. You know – gobble, gobble, gobble.'

She tore up her notes. 'I think,' she said, 'we could both do with a drink.'

'You don't have an aspirin, do you?' I asked. 'My neck's killing me.'

7

THE CURTAIN THAT CLANKS
Russia, Czechoslovakia, Bulgaria and Rumania

'I feel I must warn you,' said the Foreign Editor sternly, 'that as you are going to the Soviet Union for the first time, there are a number of pitfalls to avoid. As a journalist you are particularly vulnerable.'

'I know,' I said. 'Beware hidden microphones, women who want to get you into bed for reasons of state. If there's something I don't like keep it to myself until I get out. Be prepared for queues and lousy food, don't expect to find *Express* newspapers on sale. Don't get uptight when the wardress on duty on each landing checks your time in and out of the hotel. She's part of the system. I've heard and read it all.'

'I'm glad you've been briefed by Intourist,' he said. 'Now you can go with an open mind.'

I put all my prejudices aside on that first trip – or I thought I did. Until I found myself on my first day there in a cavernous hotel in the heart of Moscow, said to have been Lenin's city headquarters during the Bolshevik revolution. The room they gave me positively screamed that it was designed for listening devices. But how to find them – and what did I do if my instincts were proved right and they were there? Even more important, what would happen if there were visual devices, too? The KGB would thus see what I was up to. As soon as they spied me apparently ransacking the place their suspicions would be aroused and I'd be tailed everywhere.

Nevertheless, I began my task as soon as the door closed behind a dour porter. It had been my first encounter with a Russian bag-carrier who, despite all the nonsense I heard about tipping being considered decadent in the socialist motherland, had plainly lingered in the hope I would feel ashamed of the menial work I had put him to and dropped him a little something. Well, I didn't. I wasn't sure enough of myself then.

I set to work. I tried lifting the telephone up bodily, but it seemed glued to the bedside table. Unscrewing anything on the instrument struck me as far too risky – in any case James Bond obviously travelled with a screwdriver disguised as a sports car. All I had was a nail-file. I peered into cupboards, into wardrobes large enough to hold an entire KGB contingent. Moving the pictures aside was out of the question; I'd never seen such vast heavy works of art outside the National Gallery – I'd have needed the services of a fork-lift truck. Even the comparatively small frames looked heavy enough to fall and brain me if I as much as touched them. The bed was the size of a catafalque at a state funeral. It was too dark underneath to see whatever they may have planted there. I gave up. 'To hell with you all,' I said loudly. 'I've nothing to hide.'

In the next few days I mentally ticked off as non-applicable in my case all the alleged dangers I faced in the Soviet Union as a representative of the capitalist press. First, there were those enticing Natashas and Sonyas I had heard were positively queueing up to go to bed with you. At the vital moment, a photographer would rush in, snap away at our writhing limbs and the next day there I would be, standing before the panel like that child in the old Civil War painting back home. Only they wouldn't be asking me something innocuous like: 'When did you last see your father?' They would be holding up a sheaf of incriminating, glossy ten-by-eights and saying: 'One set to your editor and one to your wife. Unless, when you go back to London, you co-operate with us. . .'

Well, there weren't any women ordered to lust after me. My guide was male, a cool, sophisticated young man with English so good that he didn't even have an accent. And so neatly dressed that with his tall blondness he could easily have been taken for a Scandinavian. Which was probably why an Irish couple asked if they could share our breakfast table one morning in Leningrad.

I couldn't resist asking them how they were enjoying Russia. 'Bloody awful,' the man said. 'Can't stand all this checking up on our movements by these old bags on hotel landings with their registers. We hate queueing up for food. All that beet soup, too. And there's all the roubles we spend on excursions only to find each time that the coach-drivers say we are on the wrong bus or the buses and hydrofoils just don't turn up.'

'So we're getting out,' his wife chimed in. 'We're off to Helsinki today, thank God. We just can't breathe here.'

They finished their breakfast and rushed off. I turned to my companion who had chomped away, face expressionless, not even looking up from his plate for the entire time we were a foursome. 'Well?' I asked. 'What did you think of that for some plain speaking?'

'I think you are entirely to blame,' he said coolly. 'You provoked them.'

'Provoked them? I merely asked how they were enjoying Russia. The sad thing is, of course, that had they known you were Russian yourself they wouldn't have opened their mouths.'

'You provoked them,' he repeated. And sulked for an hour over the injustice of it all. Eventually he told me that if tourists did find some rough patches in Russia they were caused by the after-effects of the Second World War. The fact that that epic conflict had taken place before he was born was beside the point.

I went on ticking off my mental list. I'd nearly transgressed, I admit; at that breakfast table, alone again with my guide, I had to bite back, saying that I thought the Irish couple had legitimate grievances. The truth is of course that the Russians who allow us in on sufferance – because they need our money – are the last hosts who want to be told what is wrong with their tourist set-up. They can on the other hand be highly provocative when they feel liverish. But if you as a visitor to Russia want to make a protest it might be as well to do it in the safety of a group. Like the Briton the rest of we cowards in a sightseeing bus applauded one day in Moscow on one of my

109

more recent visits.

The woman guide – who looked about as sexy as the back of our grubby old bus itself – plainly loathed us all and intended to let us know it. Outside the British Embassy she lectured us on our political iniquities. 'One day your prime minister will come to her senses perhaps,' she snapped. This was stomached in silence. But when she upbraided late-comers from a shopping halt and said she wished we were Germans who were so much more punctual, our magnificent protester roared: 'Yes, but the Germans lost the war – we won it.'

He couldn't have said anything much worse in a country where the official line is that the war was won solely by the inhabitants. I'm happy to say her face went the colour of that too-frequent beet soup – and she didn't reply.

So – back to my list. Women? I repeat – not applicable. No Russian woman I have met in the course of my job has ever looked at me with 'come-to-bed-eyes', and I've certainly not met any I wished to make eyes at. Wardresses on the landing? Annoying, but you get used to it. No *Daily Expresses*? Well, I suppose you can live without them for a few days without grumbling at their absence and causing offence. Lousy food? I've had a reasonable meal or two in my time, particularly outside hotels. The trouble is that in Moscow there are just not enough restaurants. If you do find a mile-long queue for dinner you can't just shrug and try somewhere else. So it's better to book. There won't be many somewhere elses outside the dreary hotel restaurants and they'll probably be full too, with appallingly slow service thrown in.

As for those hidden microphones, if there were any in my room on that first trip I couldn't find them. I've never found any on later visits, either. Although I'd like to think that I have been bugged so that some of my verbal explosions addressed to myself after a frustrating day – I haven't made them as a sign of growing madness, but quite deliberately – might have given my hosts some home truths about their shortcomings in a more effective way than that isolated outburst by the Irish couple in Leningrad who couldn't have known they were blurting to a Russian resident.

If you choose the Soviet Union for a holiday, be prepared for rritations. But there's so much to fascinate you there – not necessarily any more connected with the triumph of communism than the Tower of London is connected with Margaret Thatcher, if you take my point – that to miss it would be to miss a unique land.

Yes, if you hit a bad day you'll be driven spare by the maddening bureaucratic delays when you arrive and before you take off for home. You might even, as Jennifer once was, be picked on as The Tourist Whose Turn It Is To Be Picked On Today. For no obvious reason other than that she appeared before the hard-faced passport-stamper at Moscow Airport with a cheerful smile and indicated to people around her that she was too short to reach even the bottom measuring line of the height-checking process on his glass screen, he refused to let her pass.

I had gone ahead of her with no difficulty. Now she was separated from me by a barrier. I was not allowed to talk to her. A jack-booted character collected her passport and marched away with it. Other people in the line were passed through from behind her with what by Russian standards was little formality. I grinned at her encouragingly and felt like death. She did her best to look indifferent and philosophical. The official went on glowering through the glass.

After what seemed ages her passport was returned and she was allowed to join me. Then came the ritual of the record of currency being carried in. Dire warnings had been given: no exit from Russia if you lost it. On this form you were to put down faithfully details of every penny you were carrying. Jennifer put down what she had: precisely one pound. The money-man refused to believe it.

'Money, money!' he roared. Jennifer produced her solitary pound note. I tried to explain I was carrying money for both of us, but was waved angrily aside. Then, in a fury, the official ordered her through the barrier into Mother Russia while he deliberately tore up her precious form in front of her. Plainly he could not believe that an arrogant capitalist could be so poor in worldly wealth.

I certainly wasn't reassured by the worried expression on the guide's face when I asked what we were supposed to do now.

111

'Very serious,' the Russian lady said. Marvellous psychology they have in dealing with tourists. Your life in their hands and so on. At last, after long anxious huddles, we hit on a solution. Moneybags De Fries would add that pathetic pound to his own total of wealth carried, and change his form to 'Mr and Mrs'. and all was well. But a lot of our all-too-short time in Moscow was wasted at that airport. And if you were unlucky, it can happen to you too. But do still go to Russia if you have the urge – I count it as an experience.

With luck, too, they may not even search your luggage when you are away from your hotel room. They certainly searched mine on my first visit – I know because Jennifer had made for me, to facilitate packing and neatness, a number of patterned zipped plastic clothes bags. These had been emptied, their contents dumped in the case and the bags themselves had vanished. (Since that first visit I have noticed that production of consumer goods has greatly increased; I'd like to think those bags represented a tiny fraction of the introductory process.) At the time I couldn't help thinking wryly of the classic Russian story of the worker who wheeled a barrow out of the factory gates each night. Each night, too, the barrow was searched by a suspicious policeman and found to contain nothing but a few whisps of straw.

On the day the policeman was due to retire, he persuaded the worker to tell him just what he was stealing. 'You can confide in me, comrade,' he said. 'I've no reason to report you now.'

'Comrade policeman,' said the worker, 'I'm stealing wheel-barrows.'

My first visit to the Soviet Union was organized in London by Intourist, to whom I paid everything in advance, including the guide, so that at no stage could it be said that the *Sunday Express* had put its unscrupulous capitalistic self under any obligation. The arrangements were made by a jovial official who telephoned me on my return and, chuckling at his own wit, spluttered: 'So you are back, and they didn't send you to Siberia, eh?'

I'm willing to bet that was his last joke. No sooner, it seemed, than he put down the phone when he was informed that, together with a large number of his mates, he had been declared *persona non grata* by the British Government and was requested to leave for the paradise he had been so busily promoting between spells of duty for the KGB.

I rather regret that he left for Moscow so fast that he couldn't even have had the opportunity to laugh at the unfortunate headline which appeared over my piece on his capital city: 'IN MOSCOW YOU WILL LIVE LIKE A CZAR'.

Thank heaven *I* didn't. They shoot czars, don't they?

The very word 'Sudetenland' has a nostalgic ring about it. You think of poor, out-of-his-depth Chamberlain in his winged collar, standing on the plane steps, waving a piece of paper and going on about peace in our time. Today, Sudetenland is firmly back in the Czech fold and you don't hear the name bandied about. And no one talks any more about Carlsbad, once the most fashionable of its spas. The comrades call it something quite different.

In what used to be Carlsbad they were selling, on my visit, roses said to have been subjected to treatment for 'x' number of hours by warm mineral water. For £2 you could buy one of these treated roses; the gimmick was, I learnt, that the colour and form would be thus preserved for ever.

So I bought one for Jennifer and I made the purchase of it the theme of my travel piece on Czechoslovakia – probably the first to appear in the West on that benighted country after the movement to give socialism a human face failed with hearty Soviet co-operation. It made a marvellous theme, that rose; the flower symbolized Czechoslovakia itself. It had been through the fire, but its old magic and bloom could still be seen. In principle, I wasn't so far out in my sentiment. Communism or no, dour Russian presence or no, Czechoslovakia is a charming little country to visit, and one day I hope to go there again.

Letters poured in from exiled Czechs. 'For the first time after so many years, I felt my tears flow.' 'Thank you for capturing the true spirit of my country.' I was both touched and happy about the article's impact. I had genuinely liked the place and I felt I had done it justice.

But after my story appeared there was one little cloud on my

113

horizon concerning that famous rose. My wife just wasn't impressed by her present. 'I don't believe a word they say about it,' she said. And Jennifer being Jennifer she wouldn't be content until I agreed that she could look into the whole question of how you preserve a rose for ever. Her method of looking was to cut the rose with a pair of scissors.

It proved to be made of stiff paper, cardboard and string. It was quite a manufactured masterpiece in itself, very skilfully done.

Only I do wish we hadn't discovered it was a fake.

A Bulgarian guide once told me that I was in his eyes a bourgeois pseudo-intellectual with anarchist tendencies. This portentous conclusion as to my character and outlook was reached after we had spent several days together. When you are thrown into the company of a complete stranger in his own environment for days on end you have to talk about something other than the tourist business. So as we drove along the Black Sea shore and then into the countryside before ending our tour in Sofia, politics and general philosophy came into our discussions and, as he told me on our last day together, he had been able to sum me up.

'I'm not sure I quite understand the description,' I said, 'but thanks for telling me.'

There was a good deal of significance in the way he opened out his thought-process to me. Of all the nationalities I have dealt with since I started travel writing, Bulgarians have been the least forthcoming, the most difficult types to talk to in a relaxed way.

It is far more common for a Bulgarian official to say, after driving twenty kilometres in silence, something scintillating like: 'Are you married, Mr De Fries?'

'Yes,' I say. 'And what about you?'

'Yes, I am married.'

Then after twenty more silent kilometres, he asks: 'How many children you have?'

'None,' I say. 'And you?'

'Five.' This is delivered with such a hopeless expression that

114

you don't feel encouraged to go on.

After twenty more kilometres he speaks again: 'You should have children, Mr De Fries.'

'For the good of the state, you mean?'

I don't know what comes over me to say something like that. It just isn't the line to take in communist countries. It plunges your host into deep thoughts, I am sure, concerning the possibilities of his having his leg pulled. Thus silence falls again.

So the character who told me I was a bourgeois pseudo-whatnot can thus be seen to be an unusually chatty character for his race. Not to say his political system.

Bulgaria is of course a country apart. It boasts that of all the Eastern bloc it alone has no Russians stationed on its soil. This the Bulgars see as a merit. The reason the Russian army isn't there, of course, is that it doesn't have to be. The Bulgarians are trusted absolutely in Moscow. Unlike their Rumanian neighbours who have done everything most calculated to madden Moscow short of flying the Star of David over Bucharest Town Hall, the Bulgarians are considered to be the last who would ever break away should the unthinkable happen and the Soviets lose their empire.

Now all this has little bearing on tourism. You can, as so many package tourists from Britain do, have an enjoyable holiday in Bulgaria. Prices are reasonable; they have done their best to make the Black Sea coast attractive. And because more Britons travel abroad now than at any time in the past and the Iron Curtain in itself doesn't stand in the way of tourism from the West – though it's a different story the other way about, more's the pity – any little lapses and rough edges on the host country's part are excused because they are what they are and you find yourself accepting cheerfully what you would neither expect nor tolerate in the more sophisticated holiday lands on our side of the great divide.

I'm no exception to being resigned to petty annoyances in Eastern Europe. But there was a period when my patience began to run out on the sort of soulless way I was being greeted when I booked into Bulgarian hotels. I would walk in, say 'Good afternoon' in English, and a stone-faced character behind the reception desk would look at me with all the warmth

115

of the *Titanic*'s special iceberg, and thrust out a hand – not to
shake mine, but for my passport. Never a greeting. Just a
rapped: 'PASSPORT!'

To the talkative and rather more human guide I referred to
earlier, I announced solemnly one day that I was no longer
prepared to put up with this treatment. After all, I had to justify
telling my readers that a welcome awaited them in Bulgaria.
'Your hoteliers on this trip are about as welcoming as
undertakers,' I told him. 'And I'm going to make a stand
against it. Maybe even start my own revolution here.'

He looked worried. 'What will you do, Mr De Fries?'

'Wait and see,' I told him.

My campaign began – and I fear, ended – when we arrived at
Sofia's leading hotel. All marble and pot plants, big foyer, and
so on.

'Good afternoon!' I said cheerfully.

'PASSPORT!'

'That,' I said, 'does it.' I looked hard at the reception clerk.
'Do you speak English?' I asked him.

'Yes,' he said.

'So you understand what I'm saying? Good. I'll tell you what
I'm going to do. I'm going out through those swing doors, and
then I'm coming back inside. I'm then going to say to you:
"Good afternoon." And you will reply: "Good afternoon. What
can I do for you?" Then I'll say: "My name is De Fries. I believe
you have a room for me." You'll look it up in your file and then
you'll say: "We do indeed have a room reserved in your name,
Mr De Fries. Welcome to the hotel. Please may I have your
passport." That is how hotels should operate, particularly one
as grand as yours. Is that all right with you?'

The stone face remained expressionless. The guide went
green and gulped.

In silence I walked out through the swing doors and walked
back again to the desk. 'Good afternoon,' I said briskly.

It was uncanny. Sweat stood out on the receptionist's face.
The guide slunk into a corner, despair written all over him.
Then, with a huge effort, the man behind the counter said:
'Good-afternoon . . . PASSPORT!'

Wryly, I handed it to him. 'Here endeth the first lesson,' I said to the guide. 'Pity it endeth like that, but I suppose "Good afternoon" is better than nothing.'

'Perhaps,' said the guide miserably, 'he doesn't speak English.'

'Of course I speak English,' the receptionist was heard to mutter angrily.

'Of course he speaks English,' I said. 'Isn't "Good afternoon" English?'

We went into the hotel restaurant for dinner. As was often the way in Bulgaria at that time, most of the *à la carte* items were off. I had a thrilling choice between roast chicken and pork cutlets. I chose the chicken. They gave me the smallest helping of chicken I've been served in my adult life outside a *nouvelle cuisine* establishment.

'Where's the child in the party?' I asked. 'Why should he be served first?'

The waiter, whose English was good, gave me an uncertain smile. I thought the guide was going to pass out.

'I'm not an ailing child with a hollow tooth to fill,' I said. 'Please bring me a lot more chicken.'

'You have been given the national portion,' the waiter said.

I stared at him. 'The what? I don't believe it. Are you telling me that there is a roast chicken committee of the Bulgarian Communist Party which decides on these serious matters?'

The guide moaned softly.

'That is the national portion,' the waiter repeated.

'Then bring me three more national portions,' I said.

'You will have to pay for them.'

'Of course I'll pay for them,' I said. 'What a boon you'd be in the capitalist world, friend.'

It was at this very moment, the guide confided later, that he was confirmed in his growing suspicions about me. I was undoubtedly a bourgeois pseudo-intellectual with anarchist tendencies.

Funny – but I'd never thought of roast chicken as character-forming.

It would be misleading and unfair to suggest that Bulgarians never have a really hearty laugh. In fact, for a week every year laughter is unrestrained, organized and even officially approved. Thus the state ensures that laughter never dies – and a good thing too.

I first learnt about this organized humour when, driving with one of the run-of-the-mill taciturn escorts through the country-side, I found myself in a small town bright with bunting and flags. 'What's going on here?' I asked.

'This,' I was told, 'is where we hold our national joke week. What a pity you will miss it.'

'National joke week?'

'It can,' he said, without the trace of a smile, 'be very amusing.'

'Tell me more,' I said, fascinated.

'People come from all over Bulgaria to compete,' he explained. 'They start telling jokes from early morning on Monday until midnight on Saturday and whoever tells the best joke wins the prize. Competition is very keen.'

I couldn't resist the question. 'What happens,' I asked, 'if a joke is told at one minute past midnight on the Saturday and everyone thinks it the best joke of the week?'

'Unfortunately, Mr De Fries, it could not be considered for the prize, as the time would have expired. So it would not be regarded as an official joke. But then it would be unlikely that the teller of such a joke would risk missing the prize by telling it when the time had elapsed for it to be regarded as an official entry.'

'The festival,' I said, 'would obviously be too well organized for such a thing to occur.'

'Competitors must know the rules,' the guide said severely.

I found the travel writer on the best of all Rumania's guided tours – on the Danube Delta from Constanta. We met in a magic world of reeds, waterbirds, thatched cottages. A special spot I have always found delightful to journey through and to write about, no matter how often I board the river steamer for another venture there. And now, to add to the pleasure of the occasion was – the travel writer, encountered by chance among

118

the passengers.

Now I seldom meet travel writers, particularly the British variety. In fact, I was first introduced to my opposite number on the *Daily Express* by a bemused tourist official on the Algarve – this was after years of our working in the same building. Travel writers are divided roughly into two types: the sort who travel in the hail-fellow-well-met *bonhomie* atmosphere of groups organized by tour operators and national tourist offices. And my kind: lone wolves who hate spending their evenings away from home on what can only be described as boozy atlas-dropping parties. 'When did you say you were last in Rio, old man? Do you remember that little place . . .?'

The travel writer on the Danube Delta steamer was of the latter variety. We knew each other by repute but had never met. Over the lunch caviare he asked me whether it was true that I was a sort of Jonah. 'I've heard terrible things about your trips going wrong,' he said.

'Most unlucky, I am,' I replied. 'There are people in my office who refuse to travel in the same lift with me. They're sure it will break down between floors.'

For a moment he gazed speculatively across the peaceful reed beds. 'Do you think,' he asked, 'that your evil eye will mess up this trip?'

'Very likely,' I said.

'Oh, what might happen?'

'Let's examine the possibilities,' I said. 'I suppose there are two – we could run aground; and we might cross the Russian frontier by mistake. I don't think it's marked here anyway. The Russian border risk is far greater.' I told him my story of the border fiasco in the Karelian forest, and of my wife's unpleasant experience at Moscow Airport. 'That, I should think, was as much to do with me as with anything else,' I said. 'If she hadn't been with me that day, the nastiness would have fallen to my lot, I'm sure of it.'

Later that day we transferred to a smaller craft for a trip through the reed beds. Within minutes there was an ominous crunching noise beneath the hull and we jerked to a standstill – firmly aground. The travel writer shuddered, avoided my eye and stared stolidly ahead. After what seemed an eternity,

119

another launch arrived and towed us off.

'One down and one to go,' I said cheerfully. He was not amused. Later he confided that he checked up with the captain, who said that in all his years on the delta he had never known such a thing to happen. He also told me that the captain had said, when confusion and uncertainty reigned a short time later, that he had never before been lost in the reeds. There had, it seemed, been a spring storm of unprecedented violence a couple of days before, and the passages through the reeds had become completely muddled – quite different from those on the maps.

My travel writer was plainly a man of deep superstition. As we went astern, turned, went forward again, as the faces of the crew and guides became tense and pale, as the most innocently cheerful passengers caught on that something was amiss and fell silent, he regarded me with an increasingly baleful eye. I forced a smile, but there was nothing else I could do.

I saw him in earnest conversation with a tour guide. 'Do you know what I've just heard?' he asked me, in a strained voice. 'One of our friends has been set to watch for the appearance of a power station. If it comes into view it means we are in Russia.' His look was more baleful than ever.

'Would that matter?' I said. 'Mistakes must occur, after all. And it's simply a case of going from one communist country to another. They're all on the same side, aren't they? The border guards won't open fire on us, surely?'

'That's not what I've heard,' he said grimly.

'Rubbish!' I said, with more confidence than I was actually feeling by now.

At that moment there was a strangled cry from the bows. Looming above the reeds was a huge multi-stacked power station. We went into reverse so abruptly that we had difficulty keeping to our seats. The boat was swung round in a flurry of muddy water and tangled reeds. We charged wildly back the way we came. Only after several tense minutes was the launch captain observed to emit a deep sigh of relief and fumble for his cigarettes with an unsteady hand.

In silence we chugged back to the spot where the river steamer was waiting to pick us up. 'I think,' said the travel writer sombrely as we scrambled aboard, 'that I'll check in future whether I'm likely to cross your path again. And if necessary, I shall have to take avoiding action. Nothing personal, of course. I shall continue to read you with interest.'

I haven't met a travel writer abroad since. The word has obviously gone round.

8

FAR OUT EAST
Laos, Thailand, Singapore, India and Sri Lanka

It was once arranged that *en route* home from Hong Kong I should drop in at Vientiane, chief city of the then Kingdom of Laos. Not surprisingly, I had never before set foot in this little South-East Asian state: It had always been very much on the outer perimeter of tourism. And certainly if there had ever been a time when it was remotely attractive to tourists, it wasn't in the least appealing when I saw it. A bitter civil war was raging between royalists and communists. Vientiane swarmed with imported partisans of both sides: Chinese, each presumably with his own portable library of the then fashionable little red books of Chairman Mao's thoughts; and patently obvious CIA agents, their pockets and armpits bulging with equally lethal but faster-acting props.

So what on earth was I, purveyor of holiday bliss, doing in such a tense place? I certainly had no intention of carrying out my normal function. I was there because, just before I left London for Hong Kong, an offer had come from the Royal Laotian Embassy we could not refuse. The King of Laos was apparently prepared to grant us exclusively his first-ever interview with a Western newspaper. From the point of view of Fleet Street, it was almost as if the one king of Siam famous in the West – the long-dead monarch portrayed in *The King and I* a century later – was going to give us his version of his controversial relations with Anna.

Laos isn't Thailand, but it presumably had elephants and

those slender dancers swaying with miniature pagodas on their heads. It was even next door, wasn't it? So it had to be good for copy. And royal interviews were not that frequent, were they? Added to that the attraction of an embattled sovereign fighting for his existence against the red hordes and we couldn't go wrong. So because I had the good fortune to be functioning somewhere nearby at the time His Majesty was willing to co-operate in such unprecedented publicity, it made good sense that I should be the journalist to do the job.

Now I wasn't too happy when, in the course of swotting up the subject before I arrived in Vientiane, I learnt the king was actually not in the city itself, but at his palace in the royal capital of Luang Prabang and that to fly there meant passing over a huge stretch of jungle swarming with red guerrillas. But I reckoned such an interview was worth the risk.

Looking back on it, I suppose I should have been suspicious about the eagerness of his London embassy to smother me with literature extolling the virtues of Laos as a tourist paradise. That stuff makes sad reading today when Laos is a People's Democratic Republic, written as it was by royalist-minded optimists without a scrap of prescience.

Anyway, there I was at Vientiane Airport, eager to see the king. I had been told that the country had a low cost of living, so for initial expenses I exchanged, at the very advantageous tourist rate, only £25-worth of travellers' cheques for Laotian currency. Just as well, as events turned out, that I didn't change a larger amount; as it was I could barely see over the top of the pile of huge dog-eared banknotes they pushed across the counter to me.

The officials meeting me shattered my illusions from the onset. 'We have arranged for you to tour the holiday facilities,' they said. I stared at them aghast. 'What are you talking about?' I demanded. 'I'm not writing about tourism – there's a civil war here, for heaven's sake. I've come to interview the king.'

'Impossible,' they said. 'The king sees no one. You have been invited here as a travel specialist to write an article about tourism in Laos. We have marvellous things in this country for tourists: lovely old cities and temples –'

'And a civil war,' I replied, furious now. 'And besides, the arrangement with your London embassy was that I should interview the king by invitation.

'We know nothing about that.'

'Then you've brought me here under false pretences,' I said. 'So I might just as well get the next plane out.'

After further argument it was agreed that more senior functionaries would be told of my views next day. Seething, I allowed myself to be conducted to what had been described as Vientiane's leading hotel. It had that faded air of an establishment which had seen its best days when the French were supreme in Indo-China. Now those not-so-secret Chinese and American secret agents were its only clients. I also discovered that a number of unpleasant-looking creatures nature had indulged with far more and hairier legs than either the Chinese or Americans possessed had already taken over my bedroom. There was scuttling activity over the floor all night – what with this and my anger at the mess I had been lured into, to say nothing of professional disappointment and resentment at having my time wasted, I didn't get much sleep.

Next morning, a huge flash American car – of the sort Bonnie and Clyde, had they been permitted to continue mayhem into old age, would have been proud to possess – drew up beside the hotel terrace where I was brooding after breakfast and a flash character in a Western suit introduced himself as Prince So-and-so. He was, he said, closely related to the prime minister, Prince This-and-that, who would be only too delighted to see me. That was the nearest I could get, he said, to a non-tourist reportage in Laos on this occasion, 'But you are a specialist in tourism,' he said. 'That is why you have been brought here. We want publicity to bring tourists to Laos from your country.'

'I've come to see the king,' I insisted. 'And only the king. I understood I was invited for that specific purpose. I'm not writing about tourism in Laos. There was no mention made of this in London.'

'You are not important enough to see the king,' the prince replied with a shrug of indifference. 'His Majesty sees only ambassadors, not journalists.'

'I've been misled then.'

125

Another shrug. 'If you can't be persuaded to write about tourism,' the prince said, 'be content with the prime minister. He is a very important person. He is in Luang Prabang and we can fly you there today. He is a prince in his own right, you know.'

'And so are you and so I imagine are most people here,' I told him.

He looked distinctly put out. 'You are not doing what we require,' he said icily. 'And that is to fly at once to Luang Prabang and begin work on seeing the tourist side of our country. You can see the prime minister, too, I promise.'

'If I see him, can he arrange to get me a royal audience?'

'Not a chance.'

'I'm sorry, but you can't "require" me to do anything,' I told him. 'I'm not interested in your prime minister, I'm not interested in your tourism. It has to be the king or nothing.'

For a moment he glared at me. Then: 'This is your last word?'

'My very last word.'

He threw a plane ticket to me. 'There is a flight to Bangkok this afternoon, Mr De Fries,' he said curtly. 'Kindly be on it.'

'That,' I told him, 'will be my pleasure.' I must say I didn't like the look on that princely face. I had an uncomfortable feeling that if I wasn't out of Laos in double-quick time I might end up encased in concrete and dumped in the Mekong river.

Without offering to shake hands, he stalked back to his mighty car.

At the airport, I handed over my huge pile of Laotian notes which seemed barely to have diminished after I paid what small expenses I incurred for my stay. The clerk in the change office shook his head. 'No dollars or pounds for these,' he said. 'And you cannot take them out of country. They must go to Bank of China, who will take up to month to change them.'

I was just about to tell him to keep the bloody things when I was amazed to hear behind me a soft, very English drawl. 'Can I be of any assistance, Mr De Fries?'

An impeccably dressed character, Foreign Office written all over him, handed me his card. He was a senior secretary at the British Embassy. So far as I was concerned, he had come at just the right moment.

'You certainly can help,' I said. 'I'd be grateful if you could take these notes and give me a cheque drawn on your account in London for the sterling equivalent – at the tourist rate of exchange, of course. And you'd save me leaving any money in this damned country.'

He wrote a cheque and with a wry expression crammed the big banknotes into every pocket he had available. 'How did you know I was here?' I asked him, curious.

He shrugged. 'Everybody knows. This is a small place. Everybody knows, too, that you intend to leave without writing anything.'

'I'm leaving because they won't let me see the king,' I told him. 'They want me to write about tourism here, with a bloody civil war raging. They must be mad.'

He shrugged again. 'I could have told you they would never let you see the king,' he said. He hesitated. Then: 'I suppose I can't encourage you to stay on for a bit?'

'Get me to see the king and I'll stay.'

He sighed. 'Impossible. But the British Government would appreciate it if you stayed.'

'To write about tourism? Forget it. You must be joking.'

'A great pity,' the diplomat said. 'But if you're determined . . .' So that was that.

Looking back on that whole bizarre incident, I'm still puzzled about what those embattled royalists thought they could achieve with my help. Did they really believe that a piece in the *Sunday Express* extolling the virtues of Laos as a tourist paradise would aid them in the war against the reds? Could they really have been so naïve as all that? And if they were so desperate to get publicity in the outside world why didn't they honour their promise and let me interview the king? As for the grudging offer of the prime minister as a substitute, why should anyone in the West have given a damn about what the head of government in an obscure Eastern country might say? Whereas a king, even if he talked a lot of nonsense, could not have failed to come over with maximum impact. Especially if he had elephants and those dancing girls with pagodas on their heads.

And what was Whitehall's involvement in all this? Was it merely that Prince Capone, having virtually ordered me out of the kingdom, had second thoughts and decided to make one more desperate attempt to keep me there by enlisting the aid of the British Embassy? Or was the Foreign Office involved in some absurd plot to prop up a regime plainly crumbling all around them? If the latter was the case, could not our people in Vientiane have put pressure on the royalists to get me into the royal audience chamber?

I shall never know the answers to these mysteries. And as time recedes I suppose I shall cease to care. But I'll always regret not interviewing a reigning king. In an age when there are more monarchs off their thrones than possessing them I don't think I shall have another chance. After all, kings don't usually get involved in tourist promotion.

Thailand may be physically separated from Laos by the mere width of the Mekong. But in terms of tourism, the two countries are a million miles apart. Thailand has a tourist trade with us that other Far Eastern destinations must envy. Britons have come to be familiar with Thailand, fascinated by the floating markets, the exotic temples and palaces of Bangkok, by the teak plantations and majestic elephants of the far north, the lovely beaches of the deep south. Also, by the island resort of Phuket. Some nervous tour operators have felt it necessary to explain in their brochures that this is pronounced 'phooket' (which can only result in ribald laughter in certain British regions north of St Albans).

We've also learnt not to whistle 'Getting to Know You' from *The King and I*, a musical about as popular in Thailand as Gilbert and Sullivan's comic opera *The Mikado* is in Japan. Nor are we encouraged by old Thailand hands to comment, when shown a portrait of that famous king of Siam, that he didn't look in the least like Yul Brynner.

The guidebooks could never say, as they do of poor Laos, that hotels outside the capital tend to be sparse and facilities are limited. You'd be hard to please not to be comfortable in Thailand. Give thanks to the American influence which shall have air-conditioning wherever it goes. And in a climate like Thailand's, air-conditioning can be a life-saver.

But Thailand has its bureaucratic side – and without the services of a competent agent, as usually provided by one of the major tour operators, things for the individual tourist or for characters like me can sometimes be a little trying.

On my first visit, I was warned before leaving London that it was vital I obtained a currency-changing certificate when I landed in Bangkok and that I ensured it contained full details of all transactions. The customs authorities would demand it when I was leaving – in fact they wouldn't let me leave unless I produced it. 'Do not,' I was told with as much hysterical insistence on the point as was stressed for the same reason before I went to Russia, 'do not, under any circumstances whatever, lose it. Or you'll be in real trouble.'

Being both highly impressionable and a coward who shrinks from technical difficulties, I repeated this to myself like a zombie and was still mouthing it silently when I headed straight for the money-changing office at the airport. But I was destined not to reach there, not even in fact to get my hot little hands on a money-changing form for the entire length of my stay.

'Where you go, Mr De Fries?' asked the beautiful creature deputed by the authorities to be my guide and mentor.

I explained. 'Money-changing form?' she repeated, the very slightest frown marring her perfect Oriental features. 'Why?'

'Money-changing form,' I said. 'Vital, they told me.'

'You no need form, Mr De Fries. You with me. Come, taxi waiting.'

'But they said . . .'

'You no need form, Mr De Fries. You with me. I with you all time. You no need form.'

'But . . .'

'Taxi waiting, Mr De Fries. You no need form.'

So Mr De Fries, throwing misgivings over his shoulder – oh naïve De Fries – allowed himself to be conducted into the waiting taxi. For his whole stay – apart from a flying visit to the north where the girl's place was taken by the Chiang Mai Press Officer – the gorgeous Thai girl did all she could – professionally speaking, that is – to see that his every desire was met and his tour went without a hitch. Admittedly he ought to have questioned to himself the competence of certain aspects of the national tourist office's personnel when he was first confronted by her Chiang Mai colleague.

'What you want here?' asked that gentleman.

'Information,' I said, rather thrown by the question. I thought Bangkok had at least briefed him.

'Please, sir, what is "information"?'

Could you imagine a press officer who doesn't know the meaning of the word 'information'?

But to return to the young lady in Bangkok. On the morning of the day I was to fly home, I was driving with her to lunch when she said casually: 'I no come with you to airport tonight. Me too busy.'

'That's all right,' I said. And then I remembered. 'There's just one thing, though,' I added. 'What about the form?'

'What form?'

'The money-changing form.'

'Ah, yes,' she said disconcertingly. 'That form. Yes, you need form.'

'But I don't have it,' I said. 'Because you said I didn't need it as I was with you.'

'Yes, you with me. You no need form.'

'But you won't be at the airport tonight.'

'Yes – me too busy.'

'So I'll need a form.'

'Yes, you need form.'

I began to feel distinctly sweaty and it wasn't just the mind-blowing humidity of Bangkok, either.

'But I don't have the form, do I?' I said. 'Because you told me I didn't need one as you were with me.'

'Yes – you no need form. You with me.'

'But tonight you'll not be with me.'

'Yes – me too busy.'

'So I'll need a form?'

'Yes, you need form.'

'But . . .' I was beginning to find it difficult to keep up the conversation, for a most ungallant, un-British desire was coming over me to throttle her – 'I-DON'T-HAVE-FORM-DO-I?'

'You not have form?'

'I HAVE NO FORM.'

'Why you have no form?'

'BECAUSE YOU SAID I DON'T NEED FORM BE-CAUSE . . .'

'Yes, you with me. You need no form.'

'BUT YOU WON'T BE THERE TONIGHT WILL YOU? SO I WILL NEED FORM.'

'Yes, me no there. You need form.'

'SO WHERE DO I GET THE BLOODY FORM?' Never before or since have I felt more like committing murder than I did in that sweltering car in the middle of a Bangkok traffic jam.

'You no got form?'

'NO.'

'You no need form. You with me.'

'BUT YOU WON'T BE THERE TONIGHT.'

'No.'

'Look,' I said, my voice now reduced to a croak and my hand gripping the back of the car seat in front of me so hard that I thought the upholstery would tear at any minute. 'Just take me to the British Embassy.'

'Why you go there – to embassy?'

'To get a form.'

'What form? You no need form. You with me.'

I gave up then. I asked her huskily to drive me to the office of the airline I was booked on. Looking puzzled she took me there. And somehow they contrived to get me out of Thailand without a money-changing form. I think they said I was a member of the crew.

I wrote in an earlier chapter that I have a soft spot for the Portuguese. My wife Jennifer doesn't have quite the same feeling for them because each time she has accompanied me to Portuguese territory – whether Lisbon, the Algarve, Madeira or the Azores – she has been taken ill. On each of these occasions, I hasten to point out, I have come through unscathed, even if I chose the same food. Nevertheless, all this has resulted in Jennifer being on her guard against anything Portuguese.

To such an extent that when we once booked in to

Singapore's classic Raffles Hotel and she heard that a senior member of the management had a Portuguese name, she sat down with me to eat in the softly lit palm court and was only half joking when she said she had misgivings.

'For heaven's sake,' I remonstrated. 'We're thousands of miles from Portugal here. And I don't suppose he does the cooking anyway – he's obviously far too grand for that.'

Next day she was feeling too lousy even to say 'I told you so'. I telephoned reception for a doctor. Half an hour later I opened the door to a smartly dressed little Chinese who bowed politely and handed me his card. I glanced at it – and did a double take.

Now it wouldn't be right for me to tell you that doctor's name. Suffice it to say that it was identical with a term which when used in a medical connotation is highly derogatory and implies the doctor concerned is a charlatan. It also describes exactly the cry of a common species of waterfowl. Presumably though, it is perfectly acceptable and everyday in Chinese.

I ushered him in. 'I see,' he said, 'you have the Joseph Conrad suite. You are comfortable in it?'

'Yes, thank you.'

'You like Raffles Hotel?'

'Yes, thank you.'

'You are a tourist?'

'No, I'm here on a working visit.'

'What do you do?'

'I'm a newspaper writer.'

'Ah. Very interesting. What newspaper?'

'The *Sunday Express*.'

'Ah so. My favourite Sunday newspaper. How many years have I read it now?'

At that moment Jennifer gave a groan of discomfort. Gently but firmly I propelled the little doctor towards her. 'There's my favourite Sunday wife waiting for you,' I said. 'Can you treat her, please?'

He examined Jennifer briefly and then asked: 'Where were you before you came to Singapore?'

'Bombay,' I said.

For a moment he looked at us both with the same expression an Edinburgh doctor had assumed years ago when I called him to my hotel and told him I'd been working in the Gorbals and felt rotten.

'Then you have caught something there,' he told Jennifer, with what I thought was the faintest hint of satisfaction. The Edinburgh doctor had used similar words and in exactly the same tone, I remembered.

'What's the trouble?' I asked, apprehensive now.

'Nothing that this' – producing a syringe with a long needle – 'cannot put right. Please to turn over, madam.'

Smilingly disregarding warnings that she took injections badly, he pumped in a huge dose of penicillin which sent Jennifer yelling halfway to the ceiling before he had time to take the needle out . . .

'She'll be all right in two, three days,' he said as she fell back in a heap on to Joseph Conrad's bed. 'Rest and quiet is all she needs. Get some sleep, madam.'

Returning after dinner in the city, I found her wide awake. 'Couldn't sleep,' she said. 'There were bagpipers screeching away in the palm court. I saw them out of the window. Girls blowing bagpipes.'

I was appalled. If she thought she heard the Dagenham Girl Pipers in such a place she must be ill indeed.

'In Singapore?' I said. 'In the palm court of Raffles Hotel?' I was convinced she was delirious. Perhaps I should call the doctor again. I felt her forehead. 'I know bloody bagpipes when I hear them,' she said crossly.

I opened the door and peered out into the court. Three Chinese–Malay girls, complete with pipes, bonnets and tartans, were strolling under the trees. They turned out to be members of a local pipe band.

'The Dagenham Girl Pipers are Malay and Chinese girls in kilts,' I reported.

'It's you who needs to see a doctor,' Jennifer said.

If I were invited to be cast away on a desert island with eight discs I would choose two in particular that I associate with my travels. One is the Factotum Song from *The Barber of Seville* to which, for want of anything better to do, I put my own words when cast away on Pantelleria:

> We are poor little *caribinieri*,
> Life so peaceful, ever so dreary;
> We are stationed on Pantelleria;
> Nothing to do but look at the sea-a.

The second is 'Raindrops Keep Falling on My Head'. Whenever I hear that song I think of India. Of a delightful hotel in Agra, where like so many visitors, I was entranced by the Taj Mahal in moonlight. I actually stayed in Agra longer than planned; flooded runways had hit the domestic air service hard. My flights to the south were delayed.

I don't remember caring that much; I enjoyed the hotel and the hotel's food. And the Taj Mahal could not pall for me. I could have listened a hundred times to the most touching of all Indian stories: how Shah Jehan, stricken by the loss of his beautiful wife, built her the world's most magnificent mausoleum, how he was overthrown by his own son and imprisoned in a fortress from where he could see the building housing the remains of the woman he loved.

The little orchestra in the hotel restaurant asked for requests. For me they played and sang 'Raindrops' – singularly inappropriate, perhaps, in view of the flooding – but they played and sung it to perfection. I sent each member of the group a bottle of beer. They played 'Raindrops' again. And again. I sent them more beer. When I went down for another meal they broke off in mid-number and changed to 'Raindrops'. Each time they saw me 'Raindrops' struck up. It became a joke with the restaurant staff. Then came a night when I had ordered a particularly delicious-sounding meal and was told before I could eat a mouthful of it that the plane service had resumed and I must leave immediately.

The band saw me get up, played 'Raindrops' in farewell and later, as morosely I ate a greasy packed plane meal *en route* south, the tune went through my head and I wished I were back in Agra, listening and feasting. I still love 'Raindrops Keep Falling on My Head'. It will always remind me of India and the little orchestra who nearly had me out of beer money.

South of Agra I stayed in a former maharajah's palace, now a grand hotel. It shone with opulence. They put me in a vast turret chamber where the great man himself was supposed to have slept. It had tiny windows, only one of which was free of the thick swathes of huge floor-length curtains which swept the whole circle of the walls. I felt stifled and tried to uncover a couple more windows. I tugged at the curtains and to my dismay the whole mass of them began falling yard by yard in huge folds all around me until the entire walls were bare. I was knee-deep in curtaining and I had to climb over a veritable mountain of it to reach my bed. Next morning I asked the hotel to give me another room. They were horrified. No one had ever before complained after sleeping in the maharajah's chamber, they said. I replied that it wasn't airy enough. What they must have thought when they saw the shambles I had created there I hate to think.

I found another former palace to stay in on my route south through India. It was grandiosely furnished with enough hunting trophies, elephant tusks and other maharahjial knick-knacks to fill a museum. But my ill-fated curtained room at the last stop was breezy in comparison with the atmosphere of this latest hotel on my programme. The outside temperature was a hundred plus in the shade, but the air-conditioning – for which the hotel charged a supplement – just didn't seem to be making itself felt.

I complained to reception. 'No, sir,' said the front-hall manager, giving a perfect imitation of Peter Sellers imitating an Indian gentleman, 'you see, you cannot feel it, sir, because it is not switched on, sir.'

'Why not – in this heat?' I asked, outraged.

'Sir,' the Peter Sellers imitation was still flawless, 'India, sir, is passing through a period of acute economic crisis. We are asked to do all we can to save energy, sir. And as there are few guests at the moment, we have switched it off, sir.'

'I'd like it on, please,' I told him. 'I don't care if there's no one else here but me; it's intolerable in a luxury hotel that you switch off. Restore the air-conditioning – or you will have one guest fewer.' I stalked upstairs. The air-conditioning was already humming away when I reached my room. As soon as

135

they saw me go to dinner, however, they switched off again. Back to the stifling room I went after dining out, found myself barely able to breathe and went back again to reception.

'Sorry, sir,' they said, before I could utter a word. 'We will switch on again immediately. You see, sir, when you went out, that left no guests in the hotel at all.'

I dined in on the second night and asked to see the *à la carte* menu. The list of European-style dishes stretched into infinity. I didn't fancy Indian food that night, so there was no difficulty getting what turned out to be a quite passable starter and main course. Good old Raj – the British–Indian tradition has its points sometimes. But with the desserts I came unstuck.

My eye fastened on 'crêpes Normande'. Suddenly I was far away from India, from the heat of the East, from the elephant tusks and maharajah's bed chambers. I was in the soft dusk of an early autumn evening in France, being served on a restaurant terrace with superb pancakes filled with cinammon-spiced apple. I hadn't eaten an apple – a rare pricey fruit in much of India – since I had come out East. Suddenly I craved for its taste . . .

'Does this mean what it says?' I asked.

The waiter beamed 'Yes, sir. Pancakes done like they are in Normandy, sir. You would like Normandy pancakes, sir?'

'You have all the ingredients here?'

'Of course, sir.'

Forty minutes went by. Then the waiter reappeared with a wide silver dish. On it were two pancakes – unfilled, completely flat. And when, incredulous, I forked up a piece of one, it not only tasted as plain as it looked, it was stone-cold.

I summoned the waiter. 'This,' I said, 'is just a plain pancake. No filling, no spices. And cold.'

He was undismayed. 'That's right, sir. We always do Normandy pancakes like this in India, sir. Plain and cold.'

'Ridiculous,' I said. 'Sweet Normandy pancakes should be hot, with fruit and spices. Kindly give me what the menu says – and don't keep me waiting for another forty minutes, either.'

He returned ten minutes later with his silver dish. Complete with two flat, plain pancakes, sizzling hot. They were plainly the original pancakes, too: one still bore the mark of my fork.

I, too, was sizzling now. 'Good God,' I exploded, 'they're the same damned pancakes heated up.'

'Oh no, sir,' the waiter said. 'That one there, sir, is fresh. The other is the one you spoilt with your fork, sir.'

Moral: don't order crêpes Normande Indian-style. Perhaps we threw the French out of India too soon.

The only fault I found with one Sri Lankan hotel concerned the shower compartment. It was open to the sky, which meant that as soon as you switched on the light every flying and crawling insect imaginable came to share the *douche* with you. Strangely enough, the hotel was proud of these open-air showers; the management considered they added a novel touch to the establishment.

I hated the whole idea. And when ants in military formation reminiscent of that airport hotel in the Azores where I was grounded so long ago marched down the walls and swarmed over everything in sight, I telephoned reception and demanded immediate action. A man came with an aerosol, gave a squirt or two, scooped up a few corpses and departed.

The battlefield sprang to life as soon as his back was turned. The uncollected corpses yawned, stretched, got up and resumed their drill, being joined by unscathed ants who had merely waited under cover until the all-clear sounded.

I spent only one night at Ant Mansions, but I hadn't seen the last of its many denizens. A few days later I was sitting in the office of the Sri Lankan Tourist Board's marketing director in Colombo. I told him about the struggle in the hotel shower room.

He was shocked – even more shocked than when I reported another hotel for giving me mosquito nets with holes and a toilet flush which fell to pieces in my hands. 'Ants?' he repeated. 'This is quite disgraceful.' He bent forward to make a note of my complaint. And as he did, I stared mesmerized over his shoulder. Down the wall of his office came – ants. Ants in the dozens. Ants in their hundreds.

I just couldn't think how long it had taken them to make that journey from the out-of-town hotel to the office in the heart of

Sri Lanka's capital – even if they did get a lift on the way.

Plainly they were there to tell their side of the story – to complain about *me*. I didn't wait to hear them put their case – the marketing director might have accepted their version of events. After all, they were *Sri Lankan* ants.

9
EVEN FURTHER EAST
Japan, China and a Little Bit of New Zealand

I just couldn't bring myself to take the suggested crash course in flower-arranging. But I said I'd watch for a bit. So I sat there in my socks on the tightly woven straw mats the Japanese call *tatami* as one lady in a kimono made an asymmetrical marvel from a huge bunch of mixed blooms. And another kimonoed beauty sat beside me with a Japanese–English dictionary ready to deal with any questions.

I didn't have any queries on the flowers. But I did venture to suggest that since coming to Japan I'd been made to feel clumsy. The lady beside me frowned. 'Clum-sy? A moment, please.' She burrowed into her dictionary, looked up, shook her head and said: 'So sorry, but no clum-sy.'

'Inelegant, then,' I said.

'In-ele-gant. Moment, please . . . Ah, so. In-ele-gant. Thank you. A compliment, I think.' She smiled. Then she saw I was committing the unforgivable sin of taking my eyes for too long off the flower arrangement and said: 'Please to watch.' There came into her voice just the merest hint of the pedagogue gently upbraiding a recalcitrant pupil. And there was a lot more of the same to follow for me that day in Tokyo.

I'd been in Japan a week already and I had to confess to myself that I was no nearer understanding the Japanese than I was when I arrived. In an earlier chapter I said that tourism as such was essentially superficial, that it wasn't my job – in any

139

event I did not have the time to make it so – to look much below the surface. But I soon realized that it was quite impossible to write a piece on this most extraordinary of all countries without going a bit deeper than usual, without trying to put across in some way what the Japanese are really like as people.

After all, what do we think we know about them: 'Dirty British plisoner must go in camp sweatbox for insolence to imperial Japanese officer.' Tourists, visiting the West, bowing and hissing, all teeth and glasses, laden with cameras, following like zombies an officious little guide complete with vivid red-and-white sun flag. Mass producers of trucks with ventilator grills looking like the self-same teeth and headlamps uncannily like the self-same specs.

I myself had fallen for the Western parody of the Japs. I'd been understandably irritated when a group of Japanese, positively weighed down by cameras and light meters, had elbowed me aside from the rail of a sightseeing boat on a New Zealand lake while they expended enough film to overload and sink an American battleship in Pearl Harbor. And even more outraged when, seeing me without the fixed grin they thought natural under the circumstances, they had appointed a spokes-man who shuffled up to me, bowed and murmured: 'We think you very quiet.'

As it so happened they had misunderstood the reason for my continuing scowl. Any irritation I had felt towards them had been momentary. It had gone from my mind as soon as they had retreated from the rail to recharge their cameras. On that perfect day in one of the loveliest countries I know, I was simply brooding, feeling disappointed and a sense of anti-climax following my visit to a lakeside sheep station. 'We have thousands of sheep on 64,000 acres,' the station owner had boasted. But I had seen only about six sheep, plainly hand-picked for the job of fall-guys to the rounding-up techniques of his collies. And our carefully devised route through the shearing-sheds had ended in a highly commercial-ized souvenir shop selling highly expensive goods and complete with the owner's wife – plainly a quick-change artist – who had rushed on ahead to dress in country costume and sit demurely behind a spinning-wheel for both folksy effect and the benefit of

140

Nipponese camera clickers.

So when the spokesman of the pushing and barging brigade on the return boat trip had pronounced that I was 'very quiet' I flared up and said something to the effect that as they were all making one hell of a noise it was as well that at least one person aboard endeavoured to create a peaceful atmosphere in tune with the surroundings.

There was another bow in answer to this eruption. And the spokesman then shuffled away to report to his cronies, who stood in wondering groups pointing at me and muttering before sending the unwelcome emissary to me again with the message: 'My friends think you too quiet for trip of this sort.'

'Too damned bad,' I grated. 'Tell them to mind their own business.' And went on sulking.

Too quiet indeed! Yet, I was to discover that in the Japanese homeland, stillness and tranquillity are all part of the Eastern mystique the Japanese themselves seek to put over when portraying their traditional way of life.

The stillness of that simply furnished villa room in Tokyo where the lovely creature in her kimono was finishing off her flower arrangement had a strangely soothing effect. The note of reproach in the voice of the lady sitting beside me when I allowed my attention to wander made me feel positively ashamed that I had opened my mouth at all.

'Now for tea ceremony,' she said, when her colleague had finished gentle labours among the blooms. I padded after her across the straw mats, feeling distinctly 'clum-sy'. In the little garden beyond the sliding paper screens a spring bubbled.

'Put on slippers,' commanded the soft voice beside me. I was wearing socks; the slippers were thonged and Japanese feet are a lot smaller than the western variety. Ever tried to put a thong between your socked toes and then walk across a rough-edged crazy paving in too-small slippers which can't and won't stay on your feet? The gentle Japanese lady seized my foot in a grip of iron and forced the thong between my toes so that I yelped in agony. Shuffle-shuffle across the rough paving went so clum-sy De Fries, the slippers skidding sideways like flippers with only the painful thong keeping them attached.

I was halted beside the spring by a small but firm hand on my

141

arm. 'First, you must wash mouth and fingertips,' I was commanded. Gracefully, she bent down, dabbed the tips of her slender fingers into the water and gently touched her lips. I tried to follow her example, but those wretched slippers caused me to all but fall face first into the stream. Impatiently I put my hands in the water and then splashed my face. 'No, no,' came the soft insistent voice. 'Must not wash all face, just touch mouth.'

'Must I?' I said. 'My feet are hurting. I find it all too awkward.'

She looked puzzled. 'Clumsy,' I explained desperately. 'Inelegant.'

Her face cleared. 'Ah, so. Then please follow.' There was a barely perceptible shrug as she spoke. Plainly she was already giving me up as a hopeless, clum-sy case.

To get into the elegant little tea house, you had first to take off those damned slippers. Oh, the relief and joy of that . . . Then you had to bend double and crawl in on hands and knees through an opening plainly designed for nothing nearer heaven than a dachshund – kimono-clad of course.

'Please to sit on the mat. No – facing that way, please. Towards the camellia. Please to sit still and study flower.'

Now, relieved as I had been to learn that your real Japanese on his native soil longs for tranquillity, regardless of the impression caused by noisy mobs of their tourists visiting the West, there is a limit to how long I can sit on a straw mat and gaze at a camellia. It was a very pleasant camellia, as camellias go; but once you've had a long hard look at a camellia in a vase it's unlikely that some awful urge won't come over you to look away from it.

I committed that sin. I raised my eyes to the elaborately lettered poster on the wall above it. A feathery touch on my wrist called me to order. 'The camellia – you must contemplate it for your mind's sake.'

'I have,' I found myself whispering. 'What does the poster say?'

She sighed, as lightly as the breeze through the cherry blossoms in the garden outside the tea house. 'It says "Today is a good day."'

142

'Is that poster always here, every day?' I asked.

'No – we change wording sometimes.'

'Perhaps "Today is bad day"?' She looked at me with reproof in her soft brown eyes. 'No day is bad day in Japan,' she murmured.

'No day?'

'No day. Now, please to turn round and face doorway over there. See, the tea it comes.'

Another kimono-clad lady arrived with a tray. She bowed deeply, set out dainty little bowls and pots and a bamboo whisk. At that moment the thought struck me that none of these ladies attached to the tea house and flower-arranging parlour were other than delightfully slender, with perfect teeth, were well above the ankle-biting height I had observed to be common among Japanese women tourists abroad. And they certainly didn't wear glasses. In fact, they were a delight to look at – and if I was honest with myself, I had also to admit that the majority of Japanese women I had seen since my arrival – whether in kimonos or Western dress – had looked a lot easier on the eye than those I had noticed outside Japan. Perhaps there was a special variety forced to travel the world and make room for their better-looking sisters in their overcrowded country.

Another gowned beauty came in, bowed and handed round tiny wisps of tissues and pairs of chopsticks. 'Please to put paper on mat before you,' the guide instructed me, 'and then use chopsticks to take little cake from tray. Then you must put cake on paper.'

There was, I fear, no way I could get those chopsticks around the tiny bean-curd cake. Sticky as the cake was, the chopsticks in my clum-sy hands just couldn't hold it. 'Inelegant, I fear,' I said. The guide smiled, neatly picked up the cake with her chopsticks and placed it on the paper at my feet.

'I have to eat this with the chopsticks, too?' I asked.

'Yes, but not yet. Wait until tea.' That tea-making seemed to take ages. Every bowl of green tea, once prepared, had to be whisked with the bamboo whisk, to the accompaniment of bows from the maker. Then another bow and my bowl was handed to me. 'Please – you must turn bowl clockwise four times before drinking. Then you must drink all in four swallows,' the guide said. 'Please – swallow. Then pick up cake – no, no, not like that. . . It must be cut in four pieces with chopsticks.'

Frankly, the task was beyond me. The chopsticks seemed to make no cutting impression on the little cake. They simply squashed it irretrievably into the paper, so that what had been a neat little round confection with a sort of icing on top was a rather unattractive chewed, toffee-like substance mixed with bits of torn tissue.

Despairingly, I turned to my mentor. She had, of course, cut her cake into four neat pieces and as each was picked up in her chopsticks there wasn't so much as a crease on the tissue paper to mark where it had rested. She was eating and drinking with the daintiness of a minor woodland character in *A Midsummer Night's Dream*.

Her face was enigmatic. I could have read anything in it except amusement. I felt more ham-handed than ever. 'Look,' I said, 'I'm sorry. This requires practice.' She finished her last tiny portion of cake, gave a weary little sigh and signalled that the ceremony was over.

There was still the crawl back into the sunlight through the dog-kennel-like opening, the agonizing putting on of those slippers, another ritual wash at the spring. Great moments still ahead of me. Don't ask how I got through them.

'What was that word?' the guide asked, as she bade me '*sayonara*'.

'Clumsy,' I said. 'Or inelegant if you prefer.' My feet hurt, my back ached. It was 5 p.m. and I longed for my afternoon cuppa. But I didn't think it tactful to tell her so.

'Ah,' she said, 'clum-sy. In-ele-gant. I always remember that now.'

'And, naturally, you'll think of me at the same time,' I said.

Tea ceremonies and flower-arrangement sessions are included on the list of arranged touristic things to do and see in Japan. You can also 'Meet the Japanese at Home'. In theory, the Japanese family chosen to entertain you speak your language and share at least some of your interests. You fill in an elaborate form giving virtually every detail about yourself down to the colour of your grandmother's socks as worn last Thursday before you are let loose on your hosts. And before they are let loose on you.

In my hotel bar one night I met a shattered fellow-Briton who was drinking to steady his nerves after his evening visit to a Japanese household had gone adrift from the start. To reach the house proved a far more tiresome operation than he had expected. He had to brave the Tokyo underground in the horrendous rush hour, change trains and then be whisked by taxi along endless suburban roads to his destination.

The family chosen for him – mother, father and two sons – had prepared a table beautifully arranged with specialities. But their British visitor was destined to eat virtually nothing. The father had about as much English at his command as the guest had of Japanese. The mother of the house hadn't spoken a word of English in ten years. One son knew none at all, and the other was still struggling with the tongue at college.

Every word the benighted guest uttered caused frowns of concentration and digging into Japanese–English dictionaries. A discussion of mutual interests proved well-nigh impossible. Awkward silences ensued.

Finally the despairing guest, wondering whether it was etiquette to be the first to start eating – after over thirty minutes at the table, he had been offered nothing – pointed feebly to one dish and ventured to ask what it was. In the middle of dictionary-aided attempts to explain he plunged in boldly and took a little portion, praying to himself that his hosts would join him and not dismiss him as an uncouth Western barbarian. They didn't join him. They just sat and looked. He sampled another dish. But they just continued to sit watching him. He swallowed the last crumb, then asked nervously and with the aid of feverish gestures: 'Only me eating then?'

At this the elder son uttered the one rounded-off coherent English sentence the guest was to hear in that house all evening. 'We are not as hungry as you,' the young man said. That did it. The guest could not bring himself to touch another morsel. And the wretched ordered taxi was late in coming to pick him up . . .

'My God, do I need this drink,' he burst out in the hotel bar.

'Let me tell you about my Japanese tea party,' I said.

145

Japan remains for me the strangest, most contradictory country I have ever visited. You admire the twentieth-century practicality. For example, the magnificent streamlined bullet expresses where, at the touch of a button, all seats, having been facing forward for the journey into a terminus, are turned around ready for the trip out. You're intrigued by taxis with passenger doors controlled by a push-button on the dashboard and with coin-in-the-slot television. By the perfect plastic replicas of complete meals to get over the language problem: you simply point out to the waiter the dish you fancy. By hotels of a standard that could not be improved in the West. By fast, efficient service invariably accompanied by an unnecessary but charming murmur from the waiter: 'Sorry you have been kept waiting.' By the way in which shopping is made easier for visitors. There's no excuse for a Western businessman wanting to take home a kimono for his wife to buy one the wrong size. He indicates his wife's height and other details on a chart and a pretty model of the appropriate proportions is produced to parade in the garment before him.

No one in this land where capitalism triumphs expects a tip – a welcome relief both from the ever-open hand you encounter in the United States and the communist hypocrisy about gratuities which pervades behind the Iron Curtain.

There are almost as many television channels as you find in the US. But switch, as I did, to a programme intended for local consumption rather than for the benefit of the big American community there and you get a shock. The very first bit of Japanese television I saw so startled me that I forgot my jetlag and desire for sleep and watched incredulous and open-mouthed.

I can't work out what the drama I saw was about – but here was proof that, despite all the Western-style opulence and sophistication developed in Japan since the end of the war, you are in a country apart with its own unchanged mentality.

A party of young girls, offended for some reason by the behaviour of a youth, seized him, held him face downwards on the floor and pulled down his trousers. Then while he screamed and struggled, one of their number – naturally, the prettiest, daintiest-looking – proceeded to kick him about twenty times

146

on his bare posterior. In the next scene the maiden was depicted as frail, lovelorn and appealing. But having seen what a virago she was minutes earlier, I could find no sympathy for her – even if I really understood what I was meant to be sympathetic about.

This odd streak of what I can only call a form of sado-masochism I found when I went to a *kabuki* performance – *kabuki* is a sort of costume drama in which the roles of both sexes are played by men. Warriors come on stage, clash, and fall dying. In order to give perspective, an impression that the whole affair is taking place over a wide area, each adult player has an identically dressed child double who moves slowly across the back of the stage and fights battles on horseback.

There is to the Western mind something faintly comic that the horses used by both adults and children are of the pantomime variety, except that I never saw a British panto-mime horse that pretended it was anything more than a couple of characters playing the front and back legs. Horses in *kabuki* move with perfect symmetry and timing, front legs and rear ones. You may THINK it funny – you'll get dirty looks from the audience if you so much as snigger.

But it's the fearfully bloody plots, explained by an English recorded commentary, which make you wonder just what sort of people these are. I fled before the end of one particular drama. A young warrior wants to be killed for honour's sake by an older man who has already mortally wounded the young man's princess-girlfriend. After much verbal soul searching, during which the younger warrior positively demands behead-ing and rejects the other's repeated offers of life and liberty, his dearest wish is granted with a clever sleight of hand. The dying princess now staggers on stage. The killer discovers she is going blind. So, to add to the charm of the whole occasion, he thrusts the severed head of her lover into her hands and while she squats keening over it he sits with folded arms muttering away about the sadness of existence.

It was at this point that I left the theatre.

'Why you bring such a big suitcase?' demanded the pretty girl

147

who was to guide me on a visit to Kyoto, Japan's former capital and the country's star tourist attraction. I stared at her. 'Why not?' I said. 'I've checked out of the hotel here and I'm going to be in and around Kyoto for several days. So of course I've brought all my things with me.'

We were standing on the crowded concourse of Tokyo's main station. 'Nobody,' she said, 'carries such big suitcases in Japan. Can you see anyone with such a big case?' I had to agree that I couldn't. The girl herself carried only a light holdall. 'You will have trouble with such a case,' she said. 'No big luggage racks on trains in Japan.'

'Even on bullet expresses?' I said, incredulous.

'No one in Japan carries big suitcases.'

'But what on earth do tourists do?'

'I don't know. But always trouble with big cases.'

'Well,' I said, 'I'm certainly not leaving my things in storage for days at a time when I might need them. This suitcase,' I told her, 'accompanies me everywhere.'

'You make it sound like a friend,' she said.

'I suppose it is in a way,' I told her, lightly. 'I call it George.'

She looked hard at me. 'You are serious?'

'Of course. Say hello to the young lady, George.'

'You want me to get porter to carry George?'

George was carried ceremoniously everywhere. There was, amazingly, no space to place him in the passenger section of the long bullet express coaches; he had to be left in the entrance lobby. I say 'he' because somehow I had almost convinced myself in this strange Japanese atmosphere that the battered fibre object bought at Woolworth's had an identity of its own. My suitcase remains 'George' to this day. When George falls to pieces another George will take his place. Or perhaps I'll christen him Fred.

What worries me, however, is whether that young woman put in a report to her superiors about the peculiarities of the British concerning their luggage.

'Ah, so. The name of suitcase is George? Very, very strange people. Not like us. So very different.'

It can't be – despite all reports to the contrary – that the Japanese have no sense of humour. But plainly they don't laugh at what we find funny. So perhaps it might be wise not to make a joke in Japan. I remember saying to one little man smothered in cameras that I hadn't realized the Japanese were photo-minded. He stared up at me in amazement. 'Who told you that?' he squeaked indignantly. '*ALL* Japanese are interested in photography. I'm very good photographer.' (They're modest, too.)

But so far as travel equipment is concerned, I can only suggest that before going to Japan you enquire whether it is possible to buy instant clothing – far easier to carry about. Surely the Japanese are just about to invent it.

I can't imagine what Mr Zhang would make of Tokyo, with its dazzling lights which turn the Ginza night into day, with its Disneyland replica, its nightclubs and sophistication. To say nothing of coin-in-the-slot television and bullet expresses with automatically swivelling seats. Or its May Day parade – witnessed by me in stark amazement – of trade unionists carrying red flags and marching in immaculate three-piece blue business suits and highly polished black shoes while a band played the 'Internationale'.

But then I'm not sure what Tokyo would make of Mr Zhang either. Mr Zhang wears the favoured Chairman Mao type of blue tunic, a cloth cap shoved to the back of his head, a welcoming but somewhat cautious smile. And, for visitors from the West to the Chinese People's Republic, a line of jokes culminating in puns so excruciating that you wince when he tells them.

Mr Zhang met us at Peking Airport and was to be our guide. 'Us' meant on this occasion not merely Jennifer and myself, but a group of British tourists with whom we were travelling. Lone Wolf De Fries had no alternative; if he wanted to see China he had to travel as a package tourist. So here he was.

And here, too, was Mr Zhang with his dreadful jokes and riddles. 'You would like to hear a joke, yes?' he would say. And the whole coachload of us would smile encouragingly and look at each other with sinking hearts, because Mr Zhang was a perfectionist when it came to English, and if the sentence he uttered was not grammatically correct, he would start all over again.

We would be praying, all of us, for him to get the words out, knowing that the sure sign of our release was the truly ghastly pun with which the story would culminate. We would agonize with each retrograde step, would long to grip his hand, look into his eyes and will him forward. (Didn't Mao talk about the great leap forward, or was that the first man on the moon?) And our burst of laughter at the end was more relief than a tribute to his wit.

The package tour we chose didn't give us enough of Peking (five nights) but a lot more than enough of Moscow (one night). I say this because, whether the Russians at the time were going through a particularly anti-British phase or our offence in existing at all was doubly serious in their eyes as we were spending most of our time in China, I shall never know. But the Russian attitude to us made the Chinese by comparison seem the most delightful set of communists on earth.

We flew between Moscow and Peking in a Chinese airliner with admittedly basic-type food and service. I was unfortunate enough to be wedged against a fat, bad-tempered American who kept wondering aloud what he was doing there 'travelling with the hoboes'. His long-suffering wife, whom he obviously tyrannized, would pass meekly over the back of her seat to him some pathetic bits she considered to be the choicest part of her own portion, only to have them all but dashed from her hand by her gracious spouse with a snarl of: 'I want real food; gimme real food for Gahd's sake!' Nothing could be done to improve his mood; the rest of us would offer him newspapers and books, only to be spurned in our turn. In fact all he deigned to read on that long flight was a mysteriously acquired copy of the *Wall Street Journal* which, with constant handling in such an unlikely setting, gradually disintegrated. Between rereading every line of it countless times he would slump back in his seat, emitting an occasional grunted: 'Oh my Gahd!'

Precisely how he fared – let alone survived – in Peking I don't know. Heaven be praised, he wasn't at our hotel – a sombre, monolithic structure built by the Russians in the far-off days when Peking and Moscow were the best of revolutionary friends, and plainly not supplied with spare parts. Hence the bath was too rusty to sit in and taps and showers continued to flow faster than ever each time we tried to turn them off.

It was also, as can be expected, considerably more difficult in China to secure knives and forks instead of chopsticks than had been my experience in Japan. Nightlife ended somewhat earlier, too: after about 7.30p.m. you had the choice of a couple of cinemas, opera or ballet. Nightclubs were unknown.

But this is no list of grouses against China. Like everyone else in my group, I was fascinated by it, was prepared to put up with discomfort to see it – discomfort is inevitable in a desperately poor country struggling to catch up. I brought home many happy memories of my all too brief stay there and I remain filled with determination to go back as soon as I can manage it.

I was touched by the friendly curiosity of the ordinary Chinese, by their willingness – as much as they were able – to extend every courtesy they knew towards us. The Forbidden City, the Great Wall, were as fascinating as I had always heard they were. Even traditional opera – although we couldn't make head nor tail of it – was worth seeing. And far from fleeing before the end as I did in Tokyo's *kabuki* theatre, we Britons were among the last to leave. Apparently the Peking audience either knew the piece by heart or were afraid of missing the last bus home, for they flocked out with no ceremony and a good deal of seat-back banging several minutes before the final curtain.

Jennifer had two problems to contend with in Peking. The first was the result of her forgetting to pack her reading-glasses. British Airways, with whom we flew on the first leg from London to Moscow, obliged with the loan of a magnifying-glass. But plainly this had too many drawbacks to see her through long flights and over a week away from home.

What was to be done? Someone suggested that we tried our luck in a department store. Glasses, it seemed could be bought across the counter. So we set out, to find ourselves in a store where the appearance of Westerners was even more of a rarity than it was elsewhere.

Despite the fact that it was almost closing time, Chinese customers forgot their own purchases and crowded round us.

Somehow we found the right counter, stacked with a positive mountain of specs. Jennifer started trying them on, squinting through them, desperate to find a pair she could at least use that night.

Anxious to help, assistants from other counters came to reinforce the salesman in charge of the glasses section. They had barely a word of English between them all, and the glasses man didn't even have that. Smilingly he produced a sight testing-card, indicating to Jennifer that she should read it. Some minutes elapsed before we could make him understand that she was unable to read Chinese characters. He roared with laughter; the crowd caught on to the joke and they laughed too.

Lights were going out around us, staff were holding doors open meaningly. While our search continued, the crowds began to thin, the shoppers slipping away with obvious reluctance. By the time Jennifer found a pair and was able, she said, to focus them on me and not be forced to back away screaming at the monster which met her eyes – for they all seemed powerfully strong – there were just the two of us, our salesman and a couple of 'visiting' assistants left.

The glasses cost the equivalent of £1.55. They were undoubtedly the cheapest specs Jennifer will ever own. But they were set in beautifully made tortoise-shell frames and came in a leather case complete with duster. And the man somehow gave us to understand that if they weren't suitable he would be happy to change them. We were bowed and smiled out into the street as though we had just bought the entire stock. Jennifer still uses those specs for close work – they are about three times as strong as her own, but they certainly tided her over on that stay.

She didn't need those powerful Chinese glasses to enable her to see through the character who caused the second of her Peking problems. He was a member of our group, an Irishman determined to make the point and thus discomfort, as he thought, our Chinese hosts, by getting them to admit to punitive measures taken against any parents rash enough to have more than one child.

He used the opportunity of question time on a commune visit to start his one-man campaign against the Chinese attitude to birth-control. He monopolized the question-and-answer session at which the polite woman director of the commune dealt with our points and Mr Zhang interpreted.

Nothing he was told satisfied our Irishman. Beard waving aggressively, he pressed on and on. Jennifer grew pink at his tone. One or two members of the group noticed and looked apprehensive. I unashamedly egged her on. When you spend most of your professional life, as I do, travelling alone and having to remember that it is not part of a journalist's job to enter into controversy, especially on such delicate subjects as birth-control, it's marvellous to be able to influence events sometimes.

Jennifer restrained herself until we left the commune and then told the Irish gentleman exactly what she thought of him. To the amazed Mr Zhang she explained acidly that she wanted the commune director to know the Irishman's views were not representative of those of British people generally. 'Please tell her,' she said, 'that this gentleman is not even British and that he comes from a tiny country where many people regard birth-control as a mortal sin.

'Say I consider him unpardonably rude and lacking in understanding in being so aggressive in a country like yours which has a very serious population problem and that I think he should be ashamed of himself.'

Poor Mr Zhang . . . He pushed his cloth cap back to an even more absurd angle than he usually wore it and did his best to keep up a brave smile. How he must have wished at that moment that he could defuse the situation with one of his awful jokes. Told at his usual speed it could at least have got us back to the hotel. But the atmosphere wasn't conducive.

The Irishman wasn't smiling. He was outraged and informed Jennifer that he expected an apology by next morning – the implication being, as I saw it, that without such a climb-down on her part, there would be pistols or swords at dawn outside the Great Hall of the People. He also told Jennifer, as though this made all the difference to his argument, that he had two children of his own.

Now, as I've made it clear, I don't normally travel with groups. I'd heard stories of friction and backbiting on group travel and here I was in the middle of it all. To me it was quite fascinating. I had no worries about Jennifer's ability to cope with a dozen Irishmen of his ilk. So it was enjoyable, I'll admit, just to sit back and watch the fun. And fun there was. The group became divided in their loyalties. There was both a pro- and anti-Jennifer faction in that coach. Jennifer did not deign to recruit sympathizers, but she wasted no time in upbraiding the Irishman when he seemed to be attempting it. 'You'll get no apology from me,' she told him.

Breakfast next day was going to be interesting, I thought. But it wasn't. The Irishman, pointedly taking another table well away from Jennifer's supporters, was heard muttering angrily when another member of the group asked teasingly who he intended to offend that day. 'It was all the fault of that ignorant little woman there,' he spluttered, pointing at Jennifer, who smiled blandly and went on with her breakfast. 'She's the escort of that man there,' he added, pointing at me. Escort?

There were no dawn assignations outside the Great Hall of the People. But there was a welcome relief from what had been thought by many before the uproar as being over-exuberance on the Irishman's part. For the remainder of our trip he was thoughtful and subdued.

As for the delightful Mr Zhang, I shall never know if he acted, embarrassed as he was, as faithfully towards Jennifer in his duties as interpreter as presumably he had at the question-and-answer session when the birth-control row blew up.

I'd like to think he did, even if the whole affair was as baffling to him as a suitcase named George might have been to the Japanese.

10

BRAVING THE NEW WORLD
– USA –

The invitation was waiting when we booked into our San Francisco hotel. A top city tourist official wanted to dine us at a restaurant where the hostess would be his public-relations-executive wife. She would 'sell' the restaurant to us as a possible venue for visiting readers, while he filled me in on the attractions of his city.

It sounded a typically American business arrangement: neat, well organized, kill-two-birds-with-one-stone operation. 'Count me out,' Jennifer said firmly. 'You'll be talking shop to her husband all evening and she'll be one of those slick, immaculate professional American ladies dripping with jewellery and she'll make me feel and look like a travel-weary frump.'

'And anyway,' she added, 'I'll bet the restaurant will be too pricey for you to write about. You'll begrudge wasting your time and we'll have a rotten evening as a result.'

Looking back on that incredible night out in America's most sophisticated city, I still can't make up my mind whether my finally persuading Jennifer to go with me was a ghastly miscalculation on my part or a strange sort of triumph in that she thus had indisputable proof that the more bizarre moments in my professional life are just as I describe them – without the slightest exaggeration. Certainly she would never have believed what happened if she hadn't been there herself. On the negative side, however, I exposed her to a situation – comical though it is in retrospect – which many wives would have found embarrassing to say the least. It made me thank providence for marrying someone with a marvellous sense of humour.

One of her initial objections was well enough founded. The restaurant, on the top storey of a towering skyscraper, could not have been more plush or elegant – and was obviously so high-priced that the tasselled card (written in French, of course) offered by the polished *maître d'hôtel* did not even list the cost of the dishes.

What neither of us was prepared for, however, was that we would be greeted by our hostess tottering to her feet in such an advanced state of inebriation that she looked a complete wreck, with her hair resembling a haystack on a windy day.

Being shown the card, too, was a mere formality. She had ordered the main course in advance: roast duck for herself, and for her guests what was described, with typical American hyperbole, as 'the flaming sword of d'Artagnan' – in other words, good, old-fashioned kebab and peppers.

She lurched into a chair beside me, facing Jennifer, who sat between her husband and a man we took to be a friend of his. Conversation between the two women was impossible, although Jennifer made valiant efforts before turning in despair to the husband's friend. It was plain the latter was embarrassed, but if the lady's husband was in a similar state he didn't show it. In fact, with what I can only describe as practised ease, he entirely ignored his wife and talked business to me. From time to time I would catch Jennifer's eye and I knew that for each of us, the evening, disastrous from the start, could only get worse with each gulp of wine consumed by our hostess.

From time to time there would be a slurred murmur from that lady, resulting in both Jennifer and the husband's friend looking at her with wide-eyed simulated interest and asking her to repeat what she said, to which there would be no response. For my part, I found it increasingly difficult to concentrate on the information the husband was pouring out to me: what we should see, what we should do in his city and so on. Only 'call-me-Homer' himself seemed undisturbed.

And then came crisis. There was a sudden squelching noise beside me, and I turned to see our hostess face down in her dish of roast duck. And there she stayed while three of us sat in

156

frozen silence with the imperturbable Homer droning on unheard.

Jennifer mouthed at me: 'For God's sake do something.' But the man who *should* have taken action went on talking. The situation was impossible, unbelievable. The thought went through my head that if his wife was allowed to remain with her face buried in her dinner much longer she would drown in an inch of duck gravy.

I looked at the waiters. But they refused to meet my eye, standing like statues, napkins tucked under their arms. I turned to Homer. 'I -er-er I don't think your wife's very well,' I said.

He shrugged. 'She's OK. Tired, I guess. Now what was I saying? Oh yeah, well – .'

The impasse was finally broken by the other man in the group. I shall always treasure the words he chose to bring Homer to face the realities of the night. Leaning forward, he asked solicitously: 'Something wrong with the duck, Julie Ann?'

The only answer he received was a gently blown gravy bubble. But now even Homer realised he couldn't let the situation continue. He stopped in mid-spate, glanced at his wife, frowned, clapped his hands like an Eastern potentate. Those over-discreet waiters sprang to life and raised Julie Ann gently from her plate. They set her back against her chair, carefully wiped her face with a napkin and whisked the potentially lethal duck and gravy away.

Meanwhile I took advantage of the flurry of activity to whisper to Homer: 'If you want to call the rest of the evening off for your wife's sake it's OK by us. I'll talk to you tomorrow.'

The ploy was a complete failure. Homer merely looked pained. 'Hell, no,' he said. 'You folks ain't drinkin' much. We were goin' to take you on to a drinkin' club after dinner in our Volkswagen.'

This was appalling. Words in letters of fire ran across my brain: 'Not on your life, Homer.' But how to get out of it? I was trying to think of a solution when Julie Ann leaned towards me and slurred: 'Giss a shigarette.'

'Sorry,' I said. 'I smoke a pipe.'

She peered blearily at me. 'Young man,' she said. 'Don't –

don't you *EVER* undereshtimate me.'

'Good lord,' I said, 'I wouldn't dream of it, Julie Ann.'

'Homer,' murmured Julie Ann then. 'Homer, I wanna go home, Homer.'

'Later dear, later,' said her spouse irritably. 'I'm talkin' business with Lewis here.'

'Wanna go home, Homer. Wanna go home. Take me Homer home.'

Homer pressed on with his monologue of things to do. The dessert was brought: Spanish coffee, a sort of glorified version of the Irish variety, in a huge bubble glass. To this Julie Ann now bent her attention – and her face. She plunged towards it, burnt her chin on the hot baked sugar around the rim of the glass and shot backwards with a sort of Groucho Marx moustache of cream added to her features.

I saw Jennifer's face turn pink, her eyes fill with tears of desperately suppressed laughter. The other guest's face was the colour of beetroot. It was quite impossible to take anything seriously now. Fighting back my own hysterics, I turned to Homer. 'I think, if you don't mind – ' I began.

Crash! Julie Ann fell off her chair and sprawled on the carpet. Again the Eastern potentate's clap of the hands from Homer. The waiters glided forward. One lifted her by her ankles, one by her shoulders and they bore her away, never, thank God, to be seen by us again.

Homer scurried off with the bearers. The party broke up in confusion. 'See you tomorrow, Lewis?' he called over his shoulder.

'Fine, Homer,' I said. The *maître d'hôtel* gravely presented a red rose to Jennifer. 'I'm real sorry about this ma'am,' he said, bowing. Something told me then that it had all happened before.

Jennifer murmured her thanks, then hissed in my ear: 'If that other character is coming down in the lift with us, don't say a word. He's probably a close friend of theirs.'

In silence the three of us descended innumerable floors to the street level. Reaching the foyer, I breathed in fresh air from the street and sank down on the entrance steps, groping for my pipe.

'Sorry,' I said, 'but I really must have a smoke.'

Our companion produced cigarettes and slumped down with a sigh beside me. 'My God, so must I,' he burst out. 'What an awful evening – what an awful woman.'

'I thought you were a friend of theirs,' Jennifer said.

'Friend? You must be kidding!' he exclaimed. 'They just brought me along to talk about hotels to you. I'm not even an American, damn it. I'm a Bolivian. I was trying to tell you both that during dinner.'

Suddenly, all three of us were convulsed with laughter.

Early next morning, my phone rang. Julie Ann slurred in my ear: 'Just in case you didn't think I did my job properly last night, I've left some information in the foyer of your hotel.'

There I found: eighteen identical picture postcards of the restaurant and two menus, the latter without prices, of course. My respect for that great American invention – public relations – soared to new heights.

That memorable evening out in San Francisco happened in 1972 when the Nixon–McGovern race for the presidency was at full pitch. Both candidates descended on the city and, unfortunately for me, Nixon chose the glass-covered winter garden of our hotel for a fund-raising Republican lunch. All unknowing, I was walking back at midday, having arranged to meet Jennifer at the hotel for lunch, when I found myself on the outer perimeter of the president's massive security net. Mounted police were holding back the crowds, helicopters circled the rooftops, and crew-cut Secret Servicemen – *Secret* Service? – were rapping into walkie-talkies and making it plain that nobody but nobody was walking an inch in the direction they wanted to take without at least taking the oath that they were not bent on violation of the constitution of the United States. As for going within half a mile of the hotel, forget it, bud. Unless of course you had a room key. Potential assassins didn't stay at such grand places. Fortunately I had mine; I flourished it, was whisked through the foyer to the elevator and told sternly: 'Go to your room, stay there and don't come out until the president has left.'

'But my wife,' I protested. 'She doesn't have a key.'

'That's too bad. There's the elevator. Get in, please.'

You don't argue with crew-cut toughs with ominous bulges under their armpits and festooned with walkie-talkies. I prowled my room, wondering what to do. There were two problems: meeting Jennifer and having lunch. I opened the window and peered down the well towards the glass roof of the winter garden where it was all happening. A stir on the rooftop of the main building above me caught my eye. I was being fixed in the binoculars of a determined-looking agent with a sub machine-gun slung over his shoulder. I froze. He sent an unmistakable signal to put my head in and close the window. Hastily I obeyed.

Now what? Somewhere in the vast crowd outside must be my keyless wife. And by now she'd be as hungry as I was feeling. I could do nothing to help, so, I thought, perhaps I'd better get some lunch from room service and hope she'd find somewhere to eat outside the cordon.

I dialled for sustenance. 'You must be kidding,' they said. 'Room service today with the president in the hotel? Every goddammed waiter is in there with him.'

I was ravenous. I had a tight schedule that afternoon and now I was securely trapped – and without my wife, too. I could just as well have been confined on nearby Alcatraz island. But in prison they at least feed you . . .

Then I remembered the note I had found on my arrival in the city. 'Her Majesty's Consul presents his compliments and is glad to be of service during your stay.' Let's see, I thought, whether the Queen's representative carried the sort of clout his predecessors in Boston had before the Tea Party. I phoned the consulate. 'My dear Mr De Fries,' came an amused Oxford drawl, 'there's just nothing I can do, I fear. You'd need a positive battering-ram to release you from your room at the moment.'

'There's always the SAS,' I said bitterly, and hung up. I continued prowling, but keeping clear of the window. It was past two now and the lunch party would go on, I was told, for at least another hour. I rummaged desperately in our bags and found a solitary Cox's orange pippin, brought across the

Atlantic as emergency supply. It had not stood the journey well, but even the musty odour of Old England which arose when I bit into its soft flesh was bearable under the circumstances.

I switched on the television. Nixon at full spate downstairs. Peace demonstrators howling outside the hotel. Gary Cooper, looking all of seventeen, facing the hordes of Chief Sitting Bull. An incomprehensible quiz and some sort of equally incomprehensible ball game. I switched off.

At 3.30p.m. a waiter arrived with a hamburger. I fell on it like a man possessed.

Ten minutes later Jennifer came. 'I've had a marvellous lunch,' she told me serenely. 'They wouldn't let me into the hotel through the front entrance – *of course* I got as far as that. Whyever not? When I found the street door of the hotel coffee shop unlocked I went in there, intending to get through to the foyer. But the inner door was guarded. So I just stayed in the coffee shop and ordered food – piles of it. There was nothing else to do. I had the place to myself – service was terrific. Shall I tell you what I had?'

'No,' I said.

She told me she had eaten to bursting point, then decided to stroll outside and see the fun. She was carrying a long, rolled-up poster in a cardboard container – about the length of a rifle. The crew-cut brigade did not give her or it a second glance. (Their colleagues who had let her approach the front entrance of the hotel before lunch had also ignored what she was carrying.) Beside the coffee shop she had just left was the hotel's trade entrance, with barely a guard near it.

From the distant front of the hotel came a sudden roaring noice – the Republican supporters and the anti-war demonstrators were in full throat as the presidential cavalcade swept away – without Nixon. They were cheering and cursing his decoy as the president himself drove out of the trade entrance, passing within inches of Jennifer, who was still clutching her sinister-looking package.

'And nobody checked you, nobody noticed?' I asked, incredulous.

'One man went a bit pale and told me not to wave it about.'

161

Her luck – if you can call it luck – persisted that same night. We had dined at Fisherman's Wharf. I had stayed behind to settle the bill and she was walking down the stairs when the Democrats arrived. Suddenly, the staircase was blocked, lined by wellwishers as McGovern and Hubert Humphrey came up from the street, shaking hands with everyone, saying in a mechanical way with each grip: 'How are yah? How are yah?' Jennifer's hand was gripped, too, and she responded in her best Home Counties voice: 'I'm very well, thank you,' but she didn't think they heard her.

By the time I joined her at the foot of the stairs, the celebrities had gone. But their supporters were jamming the street in their thousands, and I quailed at the prospect of forcing a passage through them. I was about to suggest that we returned upstairs for another coffee until things had quietened down when a girl in front of us rolled her eyes to heaven and fainted. A burly policeman seized her, held her over his head like a doll and roared to the crowd to make way.

'Quick,' Jennifer said, 'grab my belt at the back and hang on. We're with her!' she yelled above the hubbub. 'Stick with me, lady!' shouted the policeman. Jennifer grasped the back of *his* belt and we charged through before the passageway could close again.

'Ambulance!' bellowed the officer. In seconds we were out of the crowd. Jennifer let go the policeman's belt, we spotted a taxi and both of us piled in.

'Where to, folks?' the driver asked.

'Somewhere non-political, please,' I said.

People who say dismissively that they have no desire to see America annoy me as much as do those businessmen who make flying visits there, are entertained at high-priced mock-European establishments with twee names like the Silken Tortoise and staffed by patently Irish-descended waiters who call you '*m'sieur*', and then come home and say American food is awful. Forget Europe-style eating, eat real American fare in a real American atmosphere, and above all, don't despise fast-food establishments.

You'll save yourself a fortune and return with memories of marvellous breakfasts, the best, juiciest and biggest steaks you've ever known, sandwiches I can only describe as a meal in themselves, hamburgers which make our pathetic skimpy variety look and taste like face flannel, and ice-cream creations entirely beyond the ken of the British catering industry. I don't in turn despise those fast-food places now springing up in London and certain other major cities in which American concerns have a direct interest; but there are still not enough of them to make a full impact.

Across the Atlantic there's no disgrace in requesting up to four spoons enabling a whole family to tuck into one portion of banana split as served by my own particular favourite fast-eating chain, or for asking for a doggy bag if you can't get through all the goodies provided. I've yet to find on the continent of Europe any apple pie to beat the deep-dish variety they serve in Washington and the southern states. Or a sandwich to beat the sheer delight of hot pastrami on rye.

Admittedly your first contact with the US – particularly if, as was the case with me, you find yourself bewildered by the sheer size and pace of New York City – can be a trifle off-putting. You don't expect a British bobbie to snarl: 'Get yahself a map, bud' when you ask directions. Nor when you venture into a hamburger bar and order your first American fast-food meal are you prepared for the chap behind the counter to stare at you and rap out: 'Say dat again!'

I did repeat my order on my first visit, when I had yet to learn that abrasive New York City was no more representative of the USA as a whole than London is of Britain. The response was an exaggerated imitation of my British tones, accompanied by a little shuffling dance and camp twirls of the head and hands.

'Ah say! Just listen to him. "Please may Ah haave a haamborgah and a cup of cawfee." Where you from – Mars?'

Before I could reply, the situation was saved for me. A customer slouched in, rapped the counter, muttered: 'Hamburger, coffee,' and stared moodily into space awaiting his meal.

'I understand now,' I said. 'But if I tried that where I come from they'd probably say "What about please and thank you?"'

A general guffaw went up, everyone resumed eating, the

163

hamburger was out of this world – and I felt at home. I've felt that way in the States ever since – more strongly each time I go.

Even the disbelief with which the smaller, less sophisticated establishments react if the staff happen to spot pound notes in your wallet as you fish out your dollar bills has an endearing quality about it.

'What's dat for, toy money?'

'This is a pound note.'

'What's it worth in dollars?'

If you're lucky enough to be there when the exchange rate is good, you say: 'Worth a lot more than a dollar.' Or – and I look forward to those golden days returning – 'Worth more than two dollars.'

'Show.' The pound note is passed from hand to hand. The customers want to see it too. 'Worth more than one dollar? You're kidding, uh? Here, Hank, take a look at dis here – worth more than a dollar, dis guy says.'

America is a great place. As for the British who are determined to damn everything American without even going to see for themselves, I can only say they just don't know what they are missing. There's no country in the world with such a fascinating variety of scenery, of atmosphere, nowhere more packed with both man-and-nature-made wonders.

A particularly annoying snobbishness we exhibit manifests itself in sneers at what we regard as America's lack of history. Yet, leaving aside the over-glamorizing of the past by Hollywood and the absurd idea that 'real' American history only begins with the War of Independence, can there be anything more exciting, more colourful than the events which Americans have experienced and crammed into a few short years? And why *should* we smirk when we learn of archaeological digs in Virginia?

Admittedly, I have laughed at the all too frequent examples of hyperbole and downright twisting of facts contained in the commentaries of sightseeing guides in the States – although they are usually not much wider of the truth than some of the piffle American visitors to London pay to hear on Thames boat trips.

I shan't forget the guide in one American city who told his

164

coach passengers that the roadside trees were called London planes to commemorate Jack London the famous thriller writer. When I pointed out – there's a know-all like me on most sightseeing tours – that the trees were obviously planted long before Jack London had ever put pen to paper and were of the type originally placed in our capital to withstand sooty air, he replied irritably: 'That's my story and I'm sticking to it.'

I remember, too, the Boston guide who told us all about the great massacre 'when the British Redcoats mowed down the patriots fighting for freedom'.

To my question: 'How many people died in this massacre?' he said snappily: 'A great number.'

'Obviously, if you call it a massacre,' I said. 'But how many exactly?'

'A great number.'

'Tell der limey how many died and let's get on,' came a growl from the back.

The guide scowled. 'A lot of our people died that day.'

'Five, actually,' I said.

'A massacre,' said the guide.

'Dat's a massacre?' asked a wondering voice straight out of *West Side Story*. The bus shook with laughter. Even the guide joined in.

I love America.

If Boston and New England have a thing about the Revolution, the South still fights a more recent conflict: the Civil War. True Southerners prefer to call it The War Between the States. Deeper Southerners still – the War of Northern Aggression. They admit they lost – but they lost gallantly, they say.

The territory of the old Confederacy has given me some of my most enchanting American memories; there are few cities anywhere in the world more beautiful to my eyes than Savannah and Charleston – it was in Charleston Harbour, at Fort Sumter, that the Civil War erupted. You're unlikely to hear anything short of pinpoint accuracy about that war at its very birthplace, but facts do get somewhat strained in the telling elsewhere in the South and I sometimes think their tourist industry is not that well informed.

Once Louisiana was content to regale its visitors with jazz in New Orleans and paddle-steamer trips up the Mississippi. But, with the influx of tourists from Europe, the state is exploiting its other assets. Those magnificent colonnaded mansions on the river banks, once the homes of plantation slave-owners, are being bought back from the commercial companies which had used them as offices and the buildings are now being restored to their former glories.

It was at one of the most impressive of these mansions that I met Mary Lou. I won't tell you her real name – it would be unfair because such was her enthusiasm for the Old Cause that I am sure she is still as active today in keeping the Stars and Bars flying as she was when I was there a few years ago and it would bring back to her a painful memory of how a British visitor – with the best of intentions, I may say – ruined her day and her dreams.

Suffice it to say that Mary Lou was one of the most generously proportioned ladies I have ever met and that her surname could not have been less apt for someone of her size. She greeted me on the wide porch dressed in 1860s costume, with great pink arms like hams bursting from short frilly sleeves and the full skirt if anything making her look even larger than she actually was – certainly not in the least like Scarlett O'Hara. She was there to show visitors around the house for a fee to be used towards the cost of its restoration. Many of the rooms were still in debris-strewn shambles, and there were gaps in the plasterwork of the outer walls.

It was only after I had remarked casually that the British name of the materials used in the building of the walls was wattle-and-daub that it dawned on her I was from across the Atlantic.

'Ah just loves your royalty,' she gushed.

'I'm so glad,' I said politely. 'Anyone in particular – the Queen, maybe?'

'Waal, not the Queen first and foremost, lovely and gracious lady though she is,' said Mary Lou. 'Mah own favourite is Prince Albert.'

'You mean Prince Philip.'

'No – ah mean Prince Albert.'

166

'Queen Victoria's husband? But he's been dead a long time,' I said.

'So he has – more's the pity. But Ah just loves that man.'

'Why?' I asked, intrigued.

'Because,' said Mary Lou, 'Prince Albert to me is the very personification of the English gennelman.'

'Oh lord,' I said. 'I've very bad news for you. For one thing, he was German.'

She stiffened. 'German? Ah you serious, sir? Ah you tellin' me he was a Kraut?'

'Well, a German anyway,' I said.

'Mah good God,' said Mary Lou, shocked.

'And for another,' I went on relentlessly, 'if it hadn't been for Prince Albert Britain might well have gone in on the side of your Southern States and you would most probably have won the War of Northern Aggression and not Abraham Lincoln.'

For one moment I thought she was going to burst into tears. Or, in view of the period of the costume she was wearing, have at the very least a fit of the vapours. She gulped and went pink.

'Ah you tellin' me,' she said after a moment's sticken pause, 'ah you tellin' me, sir, that he was not only a Kraut, but a Yankee Kraut?' A shudder went through her large frame as she uttered the dread word 'Yankee'.

'Well,' I said, choosing my words with care, 'let's say he had some pro-Northern sympathies and didn't want to get involved in your struggle.'

'He was just a damned Yankee Kraut after all,' said Mary Lou, wonderingly. 'Just think of that. Mah idol has feet of clay. Ah'm shattered, sir, shattered.'

'He was a very sincere man,' I said. But she brushed the sentiment aside. 'You know, sir, Ah've just got to tell mah husband what you said. Right now.'

She reached for a courtesy phone without which no Southern slave-owner's mansion is complete in these ungracious times. 'Can't it wait until tonight?' I asked, astonished. 'After all, it was a long time ago.'

'No, sir,' she said firmly. 'It just won't wait, that noos of yours. You see, my husband's a damned Yankee Kraut like Albert. Comes from Illinois.'

She picked up the phone. 'That you, honey? This is Mary Lou. Ah've an English Gennelman here who knows more about our history than Ah know myself. He tells me that mah beloved Prince Albert was a Yankee Kraut – just like you. Ah'll be home late tonight. 'Bye, honey.'

11
PERILS ON MY PATH
Home and Abroad

The day I was told that only pregnant mosquitoes bite was the day I took a solemn oath never again to support women's charities – I decided I had given more than my share over the years. Like Attila I've left blood throughout foreign parts, although in my case, the blood has been strictly my own. If there is one mosquito within a hundred miles it (she) finds me. Nothing keeps her away: I have tried repellent cream, sprays, devices alleged to emit minute electronic waves, others said to imitate the voice of the male mosquito. Even the nets provided for my bed in various tropical places without air-conditioning are almost certain to have a hole somewhere.

I've developed a hatred for the smug character who, hearing of my tribulations, says with a smile: 'Funny that, old man. They never touch me. The wife gets them though, even when we're in the same bed. You both must have sweet blood, ha! ha!'

The list of locations where I've been savaged stretches into infinity. I've been pounced on along the stretch of coastline in the far south east of France where they've spent millions of francs eradicating mosquitoes in the replacement of dreary swampland with, to my mind, the equally dreary pyramid-shaped 'accommodation units' – the sort of monstrosities Speer might have designed for Hitler if the war had gone the other way. My life has been made an equal hell in darkest Africa, where the authorities, presumably through lack of money, have done nothing whatever to eradicate pests and where in any event mosquitoes are considered just part of life to be tolerated. I've also paid absurdly high hotel prices in the Caribbean for the sheer joy of being well nigh sucked dry by the wretched things.

They follow me everywhere. I've even had the unique privilege of being bitten in a first-class, sealed, air-conditioned cabin on the *QE2* in mid-Atlantic. I exacted revenge on that occasion and with both the corpse of the attacker and my red swollen face to prove that my ordeal was real enough, confronted my steward next morning.

He took the revelation wonderfully well. 'In all my years at sea, sir,' he said, 'I've never seen the like. Mosquitoes in first-class indeed! Do you know what I think?' His voice dropped to a confidential murmur. 'It must have come in when the ship was in port.'

'Do you know what *I* think?' I asked in return. 'I think you're wasted being a ship's steward. Why don't you go in for entomology?'

Next to The Gambia – where just five minutes rashly sitting out on the hotel terrace after dinner turned me into one great walking blotch – the honour of heading my blood-sucking stakes must be accorded to Anguilla. To that Caribbean paradise I was sent some years ago when a rumour reached Fleet Street that the Metropolitan bobbies despatched by the Wilson government to quell a rebellion had renewed trouble on their hands.

With that close understanding of geography, so long a feature of foreign news desks to whom a glance at a small map proves that the Caribbean is little more than a puddle, London had cabled me when I was about to leave for home from Jamaica that it might be a good idea to call in at the supposed trouble spot on the way back.

The truth is of course that the Caribbean is vast and that whatever minute scrap of land in its blue midst lies astride the normal homeward route from Jamaica, Anguilla emphatically isn't it. Anguilla isn't on the way to or from anywhere. To reach it from Jamaica involved me catching three successive scheduled flights, spending a night in Puerto Rico and finally hiring from the Dutch-French Antilles island of St Martin an air taxi piloted by a cheerful local character who had done very nicely, thank you, out of ferrying dozens of reporters to Anguilla before me, bound on the same errand.

He hadn't made the trip laden with journalists for some time, he told me as we thumped down on Anguilla. That was because the trouble, as I was quickly to learn, had long before died away; every soul on the place had apparently sworn lifelong fealty to Buckingham Palace, all was peace in the sunshine, and Harold Wilson's bobbies were wondering when they would be back to their normal function of controlling West Ham fans on Saturday afternoons.

In brief, the rumours of fresh nastiness were completely unfounded. The governor of the island was amazed to see me on his little patch. 'Bit off your usual beat, aren't you?' he said. 'No tourism here, y'know.'

I explained that as a staff writer and, in London's judgement, the nearest minion to the suspected area of trouble at the time, I was expected to turn revolution correspondent if called upon.

'Well,' said the governor, 'as you can see, there aren't any disturbances. Now you have a problem of your own – how to get off. We don't have a regular air service and if you want to cable London you'll have to go back to St Martin.'

Fortunately I had taken the precaution of booking my air-taxi pilot to return in twenty-four hours and to wait around until I let him know when I was ready to leave. Transport was therefore no problem, I said. But, the governor asked worriedly, where did I think I was going to sleep that night? 'We've no hotels we could recommend to a travel writer,' he said. 'So you'd better let me put you up in my bungalow.' Then he uttered the dread words: 'By the way – are you allergic to mosquitoes?'

Even in that stifling atmosphere, I felt a chill run down my spine. 'Very,' I said.

'Then may the good lord help you,' the governor declared fervently. Poor man – he did everything he could for my comfort. He burnt flares under my bed, he had the room sprayed, gave me cream to dab over myself. But all to no avail. I had a really appalling night under his roof – the local mosquitoes must have been sex maniacs.

Having itched all the way to New York via St Martin and

171

Puerto Rico, I shivered in a blizzard in my light clothes and telephoned the *Express* local office from the airport. 'What the hell do you mean – London sent you to Anguilla?' they demanded. 'We're covering from here – always have. Nothing's going on there.'

'Only mosquitoes,' I said.

'Do you mean to say they sent you all the way from London?'

'I happened to be in Jamaica,' I explained.

'Jamaica? For Christ's sake, we could have been down from here in a quarter of the time it took you. Don't they ever look at a map? Or an air timetable? They must be nuts over there.'

'I'll tell them what you said when I get home,' I promised.

'Rather you didn't, old man.'

Still itching, I slithered over the snow coating Kennedy Airport to catch the London plane. Or at least to wait until the blizzard eased so that it could take off. Somehow I wouldn't have minded quite so much if the whole trek hadn't been a fool's errand.

Not far below Anguilla in that dread blood stakes list of mine is another Caribbean island which, while not exactly a leading holiday destination in that part of the world, was at the time at least on the periphery of tourism. That meant it had reasonable hotels and made-up roads. It certainly didn't mean that mosquitoes were a plague of the past.

That island is far better known to British long-haul tourists these days, so for this reason and another of a more personal nature, I won't reveal its name. The pregnant mosquitoes fed from me in their usual droves. They caused such alarming swellings that I had to ask the hotel to call a doctor.

The medical gentleman (white, Anglo-Saxon) then phoned me himself; he sounded like Kenneth Williams at his most outrageously camp. He wouldn't hear, he said, of my going to his surgery. 'What time do you finish dinner – half past eight, say? Well, I'll come round to you later. You won't die in the meantime, will you? See you in the bar about nine. 'Bye till then, then.'

Unfortunately for me, the bar that night was filled with

brawny airport construction workers, macho types to a man. My medical saviour, clad in tight-fitting jeans and with a stethoscope tastefully arranged to protrude from his dainty little airline bag, minced over to me. Every eye was fixed on him. 'What's your room number, then? Nine? Goody-goody. That was mine when I first came here. Let's go, shall we?'

The eyes at the bar were boring into my back with such intensity as, wishing the ground would swallow me up and with my nerves tense for the first macho snigger, I followed the doctor towards the bedrooms. Thank you, I told him, I could unbutton my shirt myself. No, I would be busy the following night, couldn't manage dinner, thanks all the same. No – I wasn't surprised to learn he had been a ship's doctor once. Long-distance routes on cargo ships, of course.

A memo to my readers: still envy me my job, do you? If you're allergic to mosquitoes I'd stick to your own line and forget it. That goes for foreign travel, too. British mosquitoes are probably more benign. I must try them some time.

There are of course other female-gender perils beside mosquitoes awaiting the unwary writer as he pursues his lonely path to find the facts to justify advocating yet another dream holiday. They are thickest on the ground – on the deck, then – when he finds himself, as inevitably he must, aboard a cruise liner.

Now cruising, if my postbag is anything to go by, is very much a matter of personal taste. There are people who hate the very thought of it, those who adore it, and there are awkward characters, previously uncommitted either way, who decide a travel writer has made the idea sound attractive, try it for themselves, loathe it and find themselves disagreeing with every word they had read on the subject. They write to the unfortunate scribe and give him hell for wasting their time and their money. No amount of protesting by the writer that he has merely given his own opinion and the facts prevailing on the particular voyage he took were as he described them, makes the slightest impression.

The writer, they say, must have been given star treatment by the shipping company. Invited to the captain's table, no less; given a posh cabin and so on. Now I'm not writing on behalf of my colleagues, but purely from my own standpoint and experience. Cruising is, as I said, a matter of taste. It is also a matter of avoiding, if possible, sailing alone, as I am obliged to do.

As a loner, you're put at tables with other loners. Soon you learn why at least a number of them are alone: no one else in their senses would agree to cruise with them. There's something not quite normal about certain lone voyagers I have encountered. But homosexuals, lesbians, dipsomaniacs, manic depressives give me no problems. It's a certain type of unattractive predatory female which worries me. To escape from their would-be clutches I have booked myself on some of the crummiest shore excursions ever devised. I have also been thrown into a panic by the very thought of losing the cabin key which alone could ensure my privacy for the night.

I learnt early in my career never to make the mistake of admitting to characters like these what I do for a living. In a trice they overwhelm me with grievances and invitations to see for myself just what an awful berth they've been allocated. 'If anyone could put matters right,' they purr, 'it's surely someone like you.' If, as is my normal practice now, I say nothing about my being a newspaperman, they sense an air of mystery about me and, purring even louder, use this as an excuse to chat me up. One virago – I can't think of a better description, for she could turn quite nasty after a drink or two – once pursued me through the ship all day and for a lot of the night, chuckling: 'Come on, I know all about you. I know you're Frankie Vaughan.'

Sometimes, of course, their unwelcome presence is just a minor irritant compared with the dreadfulness of the cruise itself. I once was unlucky enough to find myself on a Russian liner named after Mrs Lenin. With her equally unprepossessing husband beside her, she glared down in faded photographs from virtually every bulkhead. Light holiday reading available in the library consisted of official reports of the Potsdam Conference and the diary of a Stalingrad tractor-factory worker. A bullet-headed thug presided over bad-tempered

174

bingo sessions: 'Quiet at the back there. Two and two, tventy-two.' A hairy-armed transvestite repellent in a diaphanous dress and built like one of those Stalingrad tractors, came second in the competition for 'Miss Cruise'.

Riding the slightest Biscay swell, that ship had people falling down the companionway stairs. The beet soup was pouring out glutinously day after day. My bunk was so short that, despite my being normal height, I could only have stretched full length by sticking my feet out of the porthole. I began almost to feel like a British prisoner in the hold of the wartime Nazi hellship *Altmark*, straining my ears for the welcome shout of: 'Hang on, lads, the Navy's here.'

My nerves shattered, I fled down the gangway at Gibraltar and waved a not too fond farewell to Mrs Lenin's proud creation as she steamed away on the remainder of a cruise that I just couldn't endure a minute longer. And I decided that the hairy-armed transvestite, winner of the Boobski Prize, was welcome to her.

Predatory females can also be encountered on a travel writer's path over dry land. And not always by chance. There are certain members of the tourist industry who believe that a sex-sated writer will do a better job on their product. Happily and ungrudgingly, they seek to provide the wherewithal. I shan't forget the elderly, randy director of a Swedish holiday resort who, on my first evening there, waved a hand around a hotel bar filled with young blondes and announced grandly: 'You can have any one of them for the night. Take your pick – but I hope you won't go for the one I've an eye for myself. My wife's away at the moment, you see.'

'Forget it,' I said. 'I've had a long day.'

'Oh, please don't misunderstand me,' the director said hastily, 'they're not prostitutes, you know. They're working girls by day – secretaries, shop assistants and what have you. At night they're what we call wine-girls. A man orders a bottle of wine, takes the girl to his room, and if she likes him she stays. It's up to the girl – no obligation and of course nothing to pay. You see, wine here costs a fortune and any man who spends that sort of money to entertain a girl shows he is really interested in giving her a good time.

'Now,' he went on briskly, interpreting my silence for acquiescence, 'who do you like the look of among them? Just say. I'll make it easy for you – do all the talking. I'll order the wine – it's on me. Then you go to your room and I'll send the girl and the wine up to you.'

'Thank you, but no,' I said. 'I don't go for arrangements like that.'

He looked at me wistfully as though he thought me mad or queer or both. 'What a pity,' he said. 'Are you sure you won't change your mind? They'll be available up to, say 2.30 a.m. Will you be asleep by then if a girl knocks on your door?'

'With a bit of luck – yes,' I said. 'Good night.'

If I thought that Swedish character was a trifle cold-blooded in his approach to promoting his product, he was in my eyes a positively warm human being compared with the type who once entertained me to dinner with his wife in Istanbul.

'By the way,' he said casually, as we discussed my day-to-day programme, 'I've a lady for you tomorrow night. Very versatile, she is. When you've finished dinner, phone down to reception and ask them to send her up. She'll spend the night with you, but don't pay her anything. It's all arranged: the hotel pays and sends us the bill.'

I stared at him in disbelief. Somehow the whole thing seemed even worse because he was discussing it in a matter-of-fact way as part of my schedule while his wife, who spoke good English, looked on.

'Sorry,' I said, 'I don't appreciate being offered facilities of that nature.'

He looked surprised, even put out. 'Oh, come now, Mr De Fries,' he said. 'When in Rome – .'

'Look,' I said, angry now. 'I resent your taking me for granted. YOU know about it, so presumably does your accounts department. Your wife knows, the hotel knows and naturally your versatile lady knows and she's booked me for the night. I'm apparently the only one who doesn't know. You can

176

bloody-well cancel it here and now.'

His jaw dropped. His wife looked at me as if I had just landed from another planet. 'But it's all arranged.' he repeated.

'Then un-arrange it or I'll change my hotel.'

'You do surprise me, Mr De Fries,' he said hurt. 'You're the first British travel writer to say no.'

'So what?' I said. 'And just supposing the writer is a lady. You arrange a versatile gentleman, I imagine?'

'Of course.'

'And how do you explain all this to your income-tax authorities?' I wanted to know.

He shrugged. 'Oh, we just put expenses of this sort down to whisky and general entertainment.'

'Let's get down to things that really matter,' I said, fed up with the whole subject. 'What's on the menu in this place?'

'Whatever you choose, finish with baklava,' said the wife enthusiastically. 'They make it really well here.'

'Have you ever tried a delicious Turkish speciality we call "The Sultan Likes It"?' her husband asked me.

'The Sultan,' I said, 'can keep it. We've cancelled tomorrow night. Remember?'

Of course, if there is one small advantage cruises have over flying, it is that you are less likely to lose your luggage. I've had more than my fair share of suitcases going astray at airports. Try equipping yourself in the bazaar at Tunis with clothing more fitted for wearing on a projected camel ride than the suit in which I travelled from London – all I had while my bag was flown merrily to Lusaka, where it was to remain for five weeks before being retrieved and sent to my house at 2 a.m. one Sunday.

Try forming an objective view of handsome Budapest – my bag having been sent instead to Bordeaux – when the paper-like too-tight jockey shorts bought in a local store were agonizing to walk in, When the only socks available were plainly intended for midgets and kept slipping under my heel.

I was staying at the time in a Budapest hotel once gushed over by a distinguished colleague as being a little opulent enclave of Western-style luxury and convenience behind the Iron Curtain. But could I borrow an electric shaver for my £60 a night plus breakfast? 'We have only one and it is engaged all afternoon,' room service said.

'Who could possibly want a shaver for all that time?' I demanded. 'Father Christmas?'

The shaver arrived next morning with a note from the manager inviting me for a cocktail. I started on my grievances. He made light of them, professional as he was. 'If you don't have luggage, my dear sir, you don't feel the need to dress up in the evening, do you?' he said helpfully. 'As for the shaver, that was surely quite impossible. You could not have waited quite so long – not in this hotel. Watch this.' He called a minion, who delivered to us an electric shaver. 'Three minutes exactly by my watch,' the manager said proudly.

'Do me a favour,' I said between my teeth. 'Try disguising yourself as a bewildered traveller, particularly with a beard, and then see if you can do as well as that.' He looked at me, blinked, and said he would make a note of my complaint. He scribbled away importantly.

'You'll need a bigger piece of paper than that,' I told him. 'When I tell your reception that I'm in the bar and expecting a visitor, they could at least have directed him there and not kept the poor chap waiting fifty feet from me for over an hour. And when I go to your coffee shop for breakfast, I don't expect a waiter to jab a finger at me and bellow: "Remember to sign for breakfast – it's not included in the room rate." '

'I'm well aware,' the manager said, still scribbling, 'that you must be upset about losing your luggage, but – .'

'But your hotel hasn't exactly helped my mood, has it?'

At London Airport four days later, an airline official was waiting with my case, just back from Bordeaux. 'You won't have to bother to pack for your next trip, will you?' he greeted me. 'Where IS your next port of call, actually?'

As it happened, it was Bordeaux. I dared him to say that perhaps it wasn't worth his company going to all that trouble to bring the case back to London.

No chapter of perils in the life of a travel writer is complete without a reference to booze and boozing. I'm no teetotaller, but I must confess that my heart sinks when I have to deal professionally with people connected with the tourist business to whom drink is all-important. The old lady who gave Jock and me such a warm welcome in Iona, and Homer's wife who fell into her plate of roast duck at San Francisco, are just two of the drunks who have lurched across my path over the years.

Journalists, I know, have a reputation for being hard drinkers. Licensees of hostelries around Fleet Street ought in theory to retire as millionaires. But it's been my experience that when it comes to imbibing, certain members of the public-relations profession leave us standing – if you get my point. I presume that, dealing as they are with accounts of the leisure and have-a-good-time variety, they are determined to have a damned good time themselves at their client's expense.

Some years ago, a stretch of French coastline, embracing a major ferry port and a reasonably swish holiday resort, was represented in London by an elderly English consultant for whom it was the only account. No journalist so much as had thoughts of covering this territory before the PR man was on the phone offering services and advice – he must have been psychic.

On my first professional trip there, he insisted on accompanying me. He hoped, he said, that I had no plans to head straight home at the end of the visit; he had himself formed the habit over the years of staying for the night at a hotel on the British coast after the rigours of the crossing – ninety minutes at the most – and then making his way 'by leisurely stages' all the seventy-odd miles to London the following day. I suppose I should have realized what I was letting myself in for when I heard that piece of nonsense. I told him firmly that my car would be parked on the British side of the water and that he wouldn't see me for exhaust clouds just as soon as I was back. I always looked forward to my own bed at the end of each trip, thank you very much.

He sulked a little at this, plainly regarding me as a young eccentric. On our first night away he drank himself into a near stupor, then horrified me by rising unsteadily to his feet and announcing thickly that he was going to drive me around the ferry port to view its charms by moonlight.

'Oh, no you're not,' I said,

'Are-are you shuggesting,' he demanded, swaying slightly, 'that I cannot hold my liquor?'

We left the hotel bar, with me making sure he kept a safe distance from terrifyingly high quaysides. 'Let me have your car keys,' I said. 'I'll drive.' He fumbled in his pockets. He emptied them, one by one, on to the car roof in a rapidly freshening gale. Vainly I tried to retrieve the bits of paper, the tickets, maps, brochures and memos which had filled them. All flew around us and away like confetti. When the last had vanished into the night and every pocket lining was hanging inside out, he shouted: 'I'm a damned, damned fool. I've left the bloody key in my room.'

'Let's walk around the town,' I said grimly.

Later on the trip, he advised me – now anxious to see the back of him – not to catch the hovercraft to England. 'Sea too rough,' he said. 'I know these waters well. Better take the car ferry with me – even if it's slower.' Once aboard, he took a pill. 'Knock-out dose,' he explained. 'Lousy sailor – get seasick.' (He spoke in these terse, clipped tones – when sober – because he was an ex-military man. To cultivate this no-nonsense, brisk image he also operated on the twenty-four-hour clock. 'See you 13.00 hours. Right? Right.') Whatever that pill was, its effect was startling. He was unconscious in seconds.

In seconds, too, the hovercraft had hurtled past us on a sea easing rapidly into millpond smoothness. 'Damn you,' I thought savagely. I thumped him awake. 'Thought I'd tell you,' I said, 'as you know conditions on the Channel so well, that the bloody hovercraft is running after all.'

He opened one bleary eye. He looked at me in horror. 'What-wha-wha . . . ? Wha- you wake me up for? Now I'll be awake all the way across. I'll probably be as sick as a dog.'

'Never mind,' I said cruelly, 'you can sleep it off in that lovely hotel you stay in, can't you?'

Then there was the PRO who represented in London a certain British holiday island I had never before visited. He, too, insisted on escorting me personally – presumably to get the credit from his clients for having persuaded me to write about it. We were invited to dine in an elegant little restaurant high in the mountains owned by the peer who was both the island governor and president of the tourist board. I'm not keen on sherry, but he made sure my schooner glass was not wasted; he drained it after finishing his own. He also consumed the best part of three bottles of wine, and when the governor and his lady joined us for brandy at the end of the meal, he gulped down my brandy too. Then he collapsed at the feet of his aghast and embarrassed client. I was left with the grisly task of driving him, in a hired car of a type I didn't know, some twenty-five miles back to the capital on a foggy, frosty mountain road which twisted and turned at the lip of a precipice.

Somehow, despite his incoherent attempts to give me directions from the rear where the waiters had deposited him, I made it back to base and had him carted off to bed by the hotel porter.

At breakfast next morning he begged me not to crack my boiled eggs with such violence. The noise went right through his head, he said.

You really don't know what you're missing by being just a tourist.

12
BETWEEN YOU AND ME

When my present secretary first joined the office, she was nonplussed by the number of readers' letters demanding to know whether I was enormously fat because I appeared from my articles to be consuming huge quantities of food on every trip. 'How on earth do you answer them?' she asked me worriedly.

'*I* don't,' I told her, '*You* do.'

'But what do I say?'

'That, my dear girl, is up to you.'

'Well, I don't think you're fat,' she declared.

Loyally, she ignored and continues to this day to ignore what some unkind people around us would describe as ample evidence to the contrary. She closes her ears to the occasional remarks of the editor that I would do well to live on steaks (to which I reply that such a narrow form of diet would make the gastronomic sections of my articles damnably dull, and he would be the first to complain).

She replies to all correspondents that, burning up as I do a large amount of energy hurtling around the world for ten months out of twelve, I am really quite slender. *Private Eye* magazine, which has no loyalty to me or to anyone else in Fleet Street, has described me as portly. I would like to think I was somewhere between these two descriptions – despite cynical laughter on the subject from my wife Jennifer.

Actually, nature has not endowed me with slimness; it stands to reason that my job does entail a considerable amount of eating – so you must make up your own mind on the score. But the energy-burning bit is, as I think I have proved in this book, reasonably well founded.

You'll certainly not be given a chance to find out anything more about my girth if my newspaper has its way. To the many requests the office receives to publish a photograph of me, the official reply has always been that it is not company policy to reveal what a particular writer looks like. (I've always regarded this with some wryness, as the more sylphlike of my colleagues on the *Sunday Express* are from time to time accorded a head-and-shoulders portrait, if not a recognizable black-and-white drawing of themselves.)

My readers are, however, not put off that easily. What's his weight then? Does he resemble this mental picture we have of him? The latter, described either in words or by a crude sketch, has been known to be a *bon viveur*-about-town, top-hatted, treble-chinned, monocled; a stomach stretching a cummerbund to its limit, a box of cigars at his elbow.

'Oh my goodness,' says my secretary, 'he's not like that at all.' And she writes to tell the sketchers so.

What about my weight, then? The phone rings at home. 'What does Lewis weigh?' demands the correspondence editor. Jennifer does her best to oblige, adding – what loyal females I have about me! – that I do all I can to keep it steady.

It was once suggested by the powers that be, prompted by all this reader interest in my proportions, that I went to a health farm and wrote it up in my usual have-a-dream-holiday style. So I booked in at a swank establishment where most of the inmates seemed more interested in drying out than in losing weight. I allowed myself to be steamed in a fearful cabinet, with my towel-swathed head protruding like a pudding on the boil; to be pummelled unmercifully by a tiny but ferocious Japanese masseur; to exist on grapefruit (something I quite liked until then). After four days I'd had enough. They took my blood-pressure, were appalled to discover it had risen since I arrived and begged me to make it clear in whatever I wrote that I was quitting before I had given the establishment a really fair chance.

I lost a measly four pounds – but at least I was fairer to that health farm than many of its patients who stayed for the whole length of the course and slipped out each night to eat and drink expansively at a local restaurant.

Some readers are, of course, less solicitous as to my physical well-being and less filled with friendly curiosity about how I cope with the gastronomic demands of my job. They write lecturing me on being a sort of parasite – travelling the globe on my stomach while millions are starving. My conscience is clear: my job is to suggest how you can enjoy yourself on holiday and to me food is an essential part of that enjoyment. And judging by the largely friendly correspondence I have on this score, most of those who read me think the same.

I'll admit to deriving a lot of satisfaction from letters which tell me enthusiastically how the whole family took my advice on a particular trip and went to each of the restaurants I recommended – and were delighted by them all. I treasure in particular one from a man who, with his wife, spent a winter weekend in Florence after reading me on the subject, and one night found themselves in a restaurant with no fewer than four other British couples, each flourishing a copy of my piece and demanding of the bewildered waiter the identical menu. The manager, when he heard the reason for this sudden invasion of Anglo-Saxons, insisted on treating everyone to champagne.

But I was not so happy to be blasted by one indignant lady who, with a woman companion, followed my trail on a winter break in Paris and found themselves being solicited by men in parked cars the length of the street they had to walk to a De-Fries-recommended Saturday dinner. They were both so horrified, she wrote, that they turned back and fled dinnerless. She would, she said, never take my advice again.

All I could do was to write back saying I was sorry if their Saturday night in Paris was marred by anything I had written, but that if she had asked where she could eat well in London, I might have suggested a West End restaurant where the risk of being leered at by kerb-crawlers could be equally great.

'You have simply missed a good meal,' I told her. 'It would have been worth all the the annoyance.'

Sometimes, too, I have become my own victim, as it were. After all, I can only describe a meal as it was served to me on a particular occasion. I can't be responsible for changes in ownership at the restaurant, of replaced chefs, for exchange rates and inflation, of the seasonal fluctuations of ingredient costs and so on. But there I was, in a British holiday resort restaurant, startled to see a facsimile of a previous complimentary write-up of mine on the place reproduced on the underside of the table-mat – and having taken my own advice and ordered the same thing again, I found the results unpalatable to say the least. It transpired that the chef indeed had been changed. Thank heaven the restaurant did not recognize me. I told them I would never again take the advice of Lewis De Fries, despite being a regular reader of his. With a bit of luck they may by now have changed that table-mat.

I seem over the years to have become so associated in readers' minds with eating that the subject of food even creeps into letters not intended to deal with food at all. I remember one which reached me after an article on Lorraine. Was there an inclusive tour, I was asked solemnly, to Quiche? Quiche sounded terrific from my description.

It also intrudes into my private life to a disconcerting degree. During a spell in hospital, I was aroused by a cheerful bellow, echoing down the whole length of the ward, from the doctor on his rounds. 'I'll be with you in a minute, Mr Lewis De Fries. I know all about you – you're the man who goes to Paris and eats himself silly "for just £25" when it's more likely to be £250.'

Well, I certainly wasn't going to eat myself silly in that hospital. This fact greatly dismayed the fattest nurse on the staff. 'My husband,' she confided in a whisper one night, 'is very worried about you. He says that if we're feeding you on the stuff we give the rest of the patients, you'll die and then we won't get any good holiday advice. So he's insisted on my giving you this.' And she thrust surreptitiously into my locker a huge portion of her home-made bread pudding.

At one time, before fanaticism took so much of the gloss out of Irish holidays, I had a less then ardent fan in the republic who would all but call up the hated ghost of Cromwell in his furious letters to me on the subject of horse-drawn caravans. Each time I referred to them, he would accuse me of seeking, as a typical

English journalist, to denigrate his country, to pretend it was generations behind the times.

On the last occasion we corresponded on this theme, I replied that, as I threaded my way through a whole procession of horse-drawn caravans – provided for holidaymakers by his own government's tourist board – I had commented to a board representative sitting beside me that I would undoubtedly be criticized for mentioning the subject in my forthcoming piece. 'They don't exist,' I had told the bemused official. 'Your fellow-countrymen say they don't.'

I relish far more the memory of a letter from a man who told me he was 'fascinated by my articles on Bougainvillaea'. He had gone to various travel agents, he said, but they all told him Bougainvillaea was not on their books. To me the most comical aspect of it was that not one of the so-called experts in the business he had consulted could tell him that bougainvillaea – the travel writer's flower – was a sub-tropical climbing plant and not a place. I could imagine them looking it up under 'B'.

'Berlin, Bethlehem, Biarritz, Birmingham, Brussels. Sorry, sir, no Bougainvillaea.'

I confess to having two more or less stock replies filed respectively under the headings 'Nudge-nudge' and 'trams'. My secretary brings out the 'nudge-nudge' file when we get one of the inevitable letters on the subject of the genuineness of my views as expressed in my pieces, even questioning whether I really travel at all. 'Do you actually *go* yourself?' Or: 'Tell me in confidence,' – see where the nudge-nudge comes in? – 'is Blankville sur Mer really as good as you say it is, or are you paid by tour operators to promote it?'

The nudge-nudgers are told firmly that the only money I receive is my salary, that I do travel to all the places I write about and I have no shares in a travel company. I have never ceased to be both saddened and irritated by letters on this theme and it is a struggle at times to ensure my replies contain no hint of my feelings. You're supposed to develop a thick skin in Fleet Street, after all.

My correspondence concerning trams is both considerably less irritating and confined to one particular reader. We've had a merry battle over the years, that tram enthusiast and me. He

187

has never liked my descriptions of trams as 'rattling'. I have told him repeatedly that to me, trams are not trams unless they rattle like crazy – but he won't be placated. I admit that my replies have become gradually more terse in the course of time until my secretary now says merely: 'Another trams letter. Usual reply?'

The reply in current use reads: 'Dear Mr Tompkins, Thank you for your letter. Trams rattle. Yours sincerely . . . '

Of course you can't please everybody. There's the man who once wrote telling me I had put him off Europe for life. Not just Austria, mark you. But Europe as a whole. My offence had been, in a write-up on Austria, in not warning him that the mountain-top snow in strong sunshine was so dazzling that it could give him a headache; that one Alp looked very much like another; that he wouldn't get British food; that he would be pestered constantly by guides to visit *schlosses* and that one *schloss*, like one Alp, looked very much like another *schloss*. He made me feel that I owed him at least the cost of a pair of sunglasses, if not the full package-tour price.

The letters which afford me the greatest pleasure are from those who say they don't actually travel abroad but are content to travel with me on a rainy Sunday morning.

They may not do much for the travel trade, but they do wonders for my morale and general job satisfaction.

That morale of mine, you may say to yourself, must have taken a few dents in its time. What with death threats from Arab assassins, marooning on remote islands, mishandling by the travel business, lunatic drivers, dangerously maintained cars, drunken PROs, civil wars, tummy upsets, grim hotels, ghastly cruises, mosquitoes on the rampage and the rest of it. How does this square with what look suspiciously like contrived, rose-coloured-spectacled accounts which appear under my name in the paper which employs me?

The answer is that there isn't the slightest contradiction in writing in complimentary terms about a place *and* in the course of one's job, going through hell personally. For the fact is that what I write is a faithful account, as I see it, of a particular destination. And what I reveal in this book is just what happens to someone doing my odd sort of job – and I agree it is certainly odd – when things go wrong and you are involved in situations which really have no bearing on the purpose of your visit and are, except in rare instances, unlikely to be encountered by the people for whom you are writing.

Anyway, as the travel writer said on that disastrous day on the Danube Delta, it is plain I am a Jonah.

A woman reader wrote to me recently saying I must be an interesting companion on a foreign trip – how strange it was that I almost always appeared to be travelling alone. This book, I imagine, will be more than enough to put her off any such idea about me. It may also discourage those letters from women asking for positions in what they imagine is my retinue. Apparently they refuse to believe that the post of secretary or personal assistant to a travel writer doesn't positively reek of glamour.

Apart from all too rare occasions when I take my wife with me, I always travel alone. There never will be a place for another travelling companion – not even for the lady who recently sent me her vital statistics, told me she was blonde, attractive, had passport, loved food, wine and of course travel. She was forty, she said, and separated.

'Separated where?' a coarse office colleague demanded.

I explained earlier in this book that my principle is to weigh the pros and cons of each destination. If the cons outweigh the pros then I don't recommend it. In view of the absence of what might be called a crusading travel page, that principle seems to me to be as fair to my readers as any. What I cannot and will not do is to enthuse about something in which I just cannot believe, hard as I try to put myself in the shoes of Mr and Mrs Smith rather than my own. Which is why no write-up about that famous luxury train travelling across Europe or that appalling Russian cruise ship named after Mrs Lenin has ever appeared under my by-line. A few other subjects have died the death, too. I have to accept that the occasional wasted journey is an occupational hazard – although like every journalist I hate returning to the office without copy. (The office hates it, too. They've paid, after all.)

I think it was the head of the Mitford family who expressed the sentiment that abroad is bloody. I don't subscribe to this one iota. 'Abroad' can be fabulous – easily as good as people like me maintain it is when we fill the holiday columns. I wouldn't have missed these last twenty-odd years finding this out for myself in the best of all ways.

It is no condemnation of 'abroad' that I take my own holidays at home. The definition of a real holiday is surely that period when you are doing something as different as possible from the normal routine you follow for the rest of the year. So long as I am a travel writer, home is where I shall spend my off-duty life.

But when I retire I plan to see purely as a holidaymaker those places I have most enjoyed working in. No longer shall I envy the tourists I meet along the way: those with so much more time than I have to laze on a beach, linger over a meal and allow themselves to be carried away by a glorious view.

I've met many people who say they are jealous of the job I do. In these pages I have tried to show it has its rough moments, but undoubtedly it has given me immense pleasure too. I'd like to think that the good side of it has also come through.

I repeat – I wouldn't have missed it. Not for worlds.